5 MONTHS
10 YEARS
2 HOURS

LISA
REISMAN

Outpost19 | San Francisco
outpost19.com

Reisman, Lisa
        5 Months 10 Years 2 Hours / Lisa Reisman
        ISBN 9781937402709 (pbk)
        ISBN 9781937402716 (ebk)

Library of Congress Control Number: 2014954818

Some names have been changed in this book to protect the
privacy of the individuals involved.

Front cover photo credit:
Colin Hart
The Social House, Dublin, Ireland
www.thesocialhouse.co
www.mr-kennedy.com/gold

Author photo credit:
Joanne Wilcox

*OUTPOST
19*

*PROVOCATIVE READING
SAN FRANCISCO
NEW YORK
OUTPOST19.COM*

5 MONTHS
10 YEARS
2 HOURS

For Martha Resnikov Reisman

In memory of Pip

"Hell! Ever' body got scars."

—John Steinbeck
The Grapes of Wrath

Iz tsures unter alle decher.
There is an ache under every roof.

—Old Yiddish proverb

SWIM

September 2008

I

Beautiful. I had sunk $110 to wake up at 4:30 a.m. on a cold, dark Sunday morning to swim a half-mile loop in frigid waters, cycle fourteen miles, and run four through slicing winds and driving rain. Three hundred others had done the same. One had just slapped me mid-stroke in the face. Another kicked me in the gut. When I came back up for air, a hand scooped a stream of Long Island Sound water into my open mouth. It tasted like scum.

It was my first triathlon. At that moment I believed it would be my last.

As the remaining swimmers left me in their wake, I glanced behind me, hyperventilating. Whitecaps splashed against rocks; waves ripped through the slate-dark surface; the sky was a fury of grays.

Just then, the heaving waters around me calmed. In the distance I made out the orange blur of the first turn buoy. And recalled the words of the tiny, sun-wrinkled woman as we stood at the starting line, I trembling in the face of the choppy waves, she calmly windmilling her wiry arms and jogging lightly in place. "Get to the first buoy and you'll be fine," she chirped, smiling brightly, as if there were nowhere she'd rather be.

I began to regain my senses. *Just get to the first buoy.*

No way I was turning back. This was my ten-year anniversary. With life. ,

By then the details were sketchy. But I know it was a Friday night, and it was the last day of July 1998, and I was late. I had been preparing for a conference with opposing counsel to settle a case before it went to trial, and it had taken longer than expected. I sprinted across Third Avenue. The air was close.

The dark wood-paneled pub was packed. The music was loud. The group, most of them from my law firm, occupied a corner table. I ordered a Guinness and a plate of shoestring fries. Someone on the Yankees hit a home run. Everyone hooted, high-fived. There was shouting, hilarity, something about Bill Clinton's cigar. I talked for a while with a guy who had just begun his surgical residency at NYU. He was a college friend of another fourth-year associate and had curly red hair and a quick laugh.

While the bill was being split up, he asked for my number. I told him of my plan to drive across the country in a Plymouth Valiant convertible. "And I'm not even balding," I remember saying. "Cool," he replied, looking vaguely puzzled.

The streets were festive with lights. Music spilled out of restaurants and bars. It was the sort of summer night you felt the city was your own. *One more week*, I said to myself as I neared Central Park. *One week of attending the settlement conference, tying up loose ends, and life begins.* As I took in the familiar odor of exhaust and the sweet smell of honeysuckle, I felt a sort of lightness, as if something in me had opened and I could take in more air.

I caught a taxi on Fifth. It was close to midnight when I trudged the two flights to my one-bedroom and kicked off my pumps. The next morning, I went for a five-mile run through Riverside Park. It was already warm. I was spent.

As I was letting myself into my apartment, the phone rang. It was my older sister Luke calling from Baltimore; we talked every Saturday morning. I told her I needed a nap; I'd call her back when I got up.

That's the last I remember. I don't remember taking a shower, putting on a T-shirt, muting the ringer of my phone, adjusting the air conditioner to high, drawing the dark shades to block the early August glare, or stretching out on my futon. Nor do I remember lying motionless sometime Sunday afternoon while a friend buzzed on my intercom from the outside entrance and shouted my name from the patio of the garden apartment below.

I don't remember failing to show up for work on Monday morning or the spring of the deadbolt lock or the rapid clop of my stepmother's heels across my living room floor and into my bedroom early that afternoon. Or being placed on a gurney and hustled downstairs or the wail of the siren as I was rushed to the hospital or who sat beside me in the ambulance.

All this I learned later. ⸲

II

Some bodies just move better through the water. Something genetic, I guess.

That wasn't mine. Not so much because I hadn't been blessed with webbed toes and fingers, hypermobile ankles, or an enormous wingspan. It was simpler than that, and anyone who swims regularly knows how this goes. I could swim, but I was no swimmer.

That much I knew as I thrashed in the direction of the second buoy. That much I had discovered three times a week in the town pool that summer as I watched the walrus-like man with the pendulous belly sweep past me, the feet of the whippet-thin Asian girl fluttering as fast as the roll of a snare drum, the older woman with the form so ferociously perfect that she lapped me again and again.

That was hard to bear, being passed. But it was alright: this was about enduring, about finishing strong.

That was what I told myself, anyway. Truth was, I was accustomed to being out in front, vying for the win. What I dreaded was coming out of the water dead last.

Or, what would have been even grimmer: overexerting myself, growing lightheaded, flailing as the waves engulfed me, calling out for help, the sensation of darkness closing in from all sides.

3

I'd been there ten years before and I wasn't going back. Been underwater, fighting my way toward the surface, my hands and feet tied, holding me down.

Dim half-seen faces emerged and drifted off in the aquarium light. The deeply creased pouches under my father's eyes, his complexion the color of newspaper. The strain petrifying my mother's features. The solemn, bespectacled faces of two doctors who eventually defined themselves as Luke and her husband Cary.

I heard their voices, faint-sounding, questioning residents on dosages, responding to inquiries on my medical history: thirty-two years old, no previous illnesses or hospitalizations, no history of epilepsy, no allergies to medications.

"What day is this," I croaked, my voice too weak to rise to a question. "Luke. . . What's the day. And could you undo the straps."

It was Wednesday morning, she said, pushing aside the sheet and loosening the straps. I had been in and out of consciousness since Monday.

Wednesday. *Wednesday?* A chill went through me, startling me from my daze. "What time," I said, the words scraping my dry throat.

"Around nine," said Luke.

"Has someone called work?" I wasn't wondering why I was bound to the bed. I was too busy calculating how long it would take to get everyone out of the room, pull together an outfit, and get myself to the office.

Also I needed a glass of water for my throat. And an Advil. My head was killing me.

Later that day, I awoke to a ripping sound. Something was pulling against my right ankle. Velcro. My eyes winked and squinted in the fluorescent light. They were removing the

4

straps.

I could get up now, Luke was saying as my other ankle and wrists were freed. There was enough anti-seizure medication in my system.

I must have heard the words "anti-seizure medication" but I was struggling to corkscrew my body upright without appearing to struggle, and the meaning of the words didn't register.

I grabbed hold of the metal bed rails and heaved my legs around to the floor. My bare feet hit the cool linoleum. They luxuriated in the openness, as though released from heavy boots into a cool mountain stream. I swished them about for a while. Then Luke and my father, their hands under my elbows, hoisted me to a standing position.

I cringed. It didn't make sense, feeling like a brittle-boned old woman. Hadn't I just warmed down from my Saturday-morning run through Riverside Park?

Six steps to the door, a pause to get my bearings, and then, eyes straight ahead to the medical scale at the end of the hallway, I fell into a shuffle, leaning on my sister's arm. It vexed me, my recalcitrant creaking body, the effort I had to expend to cover a distance of perhaps thirty feet.

I was the athlete of the family, the first in ancestral history to win a varsity letter, the state cross-country championship finalist. I was the juggler, the unicyclist, the one who was always late for dinner, perfecting my jump shot or playing endless games of Ping Pong with my best friend Julie in her basement until we had both perfected a wicked unreturnable backspin.

I was the one who in junior high ran a six-mile loop every other afternoon and two decades later the forty streets and six city blocks from my law firm at any time of evening or night, raw-silk suit and stockings stuffed into the knapsack strapped to my back, cramped strides lengthening with each city block.

I reached the scale, sucking air. It didn't make sense. Hadn't I just warmed down from my Saturday-morning route through Riverside Park? My mind, panning across my memory, showed nothing. Had my brain atrophied as well?

"Again," I said, now dizzied by exhaustion—fear?—once Luke and I had inched our way back to the door of my room. "This time by myself."

Past my father I slogged; he stood against an empty stretcher, ready to assist. "Go kiddo," he sang out. I forced a grin on my face as I looked back at him. Weary bloodshot eyes belied his sunny words.

I made it to the scale and back, retired to my bed.

Sometime later—that first day seemed endless, like a flight across several time zones—a doctor swept into my room, surrounded by a cluster of white jackets. He sported a healthy tan under his close-cropped silver-flecked hair.

"How-are-you-feel-ing-Li-sa?" he asked, enunciating his words so slowly that he must have figured I was more compromised than I actually was.

"Never felt better," I said, pushing myself up. I was in the spotlight. Had to show them I was fine, that this was no sweat. Had to be the star patient, the one everyone vied to check in on, who would be remembered long after she was gone. Have you met Lisa Reisman in Room 722-A? She's *incredible*. You have to talk to her.

"Li-sa," the doctor said, evidently not picking up on my snappy reply. He cleared his throat. "You have a mass in your brain, a tu-mor," he said, his voice growing in volume. "*A tumor. In. Your. Brain.*"

"And?" I barely heard him. Anger was tearing through me. Who was this guy, addressing me as if I were some half wit?

"It needs to be re-moved. To-mor-row morn-ing. Eight. O. Clock."

"Let's do it," I shot back, as if returning one of Julie's killer serves. "Let's get it out."

III

The night before the race I had tossed about, listening to the rain pelting the roof of my cottage, the branches clawing at the walls, trying to convince myself to shut off the alarm, to sleep in, that all those grueling three-hour workouts had already shown beyond a reasonable doubt that I'd never been fitter.

As a stream of chill air blew through the screen window, I sat bolt upright in the darkness, wondering what I had been thinking. A triathlon? Why not just a ten-mile race? Or some kind of walkathon? Anything that didn't involve plunging into the icy water before the sun could rise high enough to shed some warmth—if the sun showed its face at all. Did it even mean anything, getting to the finish line? Wasn't it up to me, in the end, to opt out?

That was it: This wasn't of consequence to anyone but me. Not to mention it was hardly a matter of life or death.

6:05.

I remembered it vividly, the face of the heavy steel clock above the exit sign, its tick cutting into the early-morning stillness, each tick implacably drawing toward eight o'clock. And the smell of Lysol hanging in the air as I turned onto another broad corridor, the dimmed fluorescent lights casting a sallow glow on the waxed floors.

The slight tug from the IV catheter inserted in my forearm and attached to a bag of saline hanging from the metal rack I guided along; that hadn't left me either. Any abrupt movement could dislodge the tube, one of the nurses had warned earlier that morning as she replaced the bag. And if the tube came out, my surgery might have to be delayed.

7

I didn't want any delay. I wanted the thing out of my head.

I made my way past a fire extinguisher, a gurney, the clucking tongue of the clock gradually dying away. Except for the whir of wheels on linoleum and the low murmur from the glassed-in nurses' station, the silence was complete.

I reached the end of the hall, took another right. Craniotomy. I'd asked no questions and felt little emotion about the prospect of a major operation. If you're jogging past a snarling dog, my high school cross-country coach once said, pretend you don't notice it. Don't change your pace. Just keep going.

Just keep going, I said to myself.

I passed a wheelchair, an abandoned industrial mop bucket. Then the ticking, again. Another clock above another exit sign. 6:09.

Craniotomy. I'd heard the word the night before and couldn't get it out of my head. Craniotomy. *Cranium*: Brain. *Tomos*: Cutting. The words came back to me from my years studying Ancient Greek and Latin. Someone—Luke? another doctor?—mentioned the tumor was in the right frontal lobe of my brain. So why a craniotomy and not a lobotomy? I needed a dictionary. Did hospitals keep dictionaries?

Inside the station a nurse glanced up at me. I caught my reflection in the glass. Someone had shaved the front of my head from ear to ear the night before, but I hadn't thought much about it—had, in fact, rather enjoyed the buzzing sensation.

Until I saw myself. My forehead extended to the top of my skull. My insides turned over in revulsion. Mr. Munster. Tears sprang to my eyes.

Stay calm, I said to myself, using my free hand to wipe them away, keeping my other rigid to avoid yanking the IV. *Keep going.*

6:13.

And then I was on a stretcher and Luke was hurrying alongside and figures were fading in and out of eyeshot as in some old B movie: white-jacketed young doctor with startling eyes striding purposefully ahead; weathered old man in a wheelchair pushing himself forward with his feet; pigeon-toed nun with a kind, worn face stumping by.

"You'll be alright, Lise," I heard my mother saying from the other side. I tried to look back, but already the stretcher was beyond her and Luke.

"Wait a moment." My mother's voice calling out, strong, firm, but with a tiny hairline fracture. "Wait one moment."

The stretcher stopped, its wheels creaking. There she was, smiling, her eyes moist.

"Don't go sappy on me, Mom," I said. My voice came out crackly. I hadn't had anything to eat or drink since the night before. I didn't want to sound weak. I wanted to sound brave. "I'll be fine.".

And finally the murmur of voices, the click of metal instruments, coffee breath. A pair of crinkly eyes beneath a paisley surgical cap replacing the saucer-shaped lights staring down at me. "All set, Lisa?" asked a roundish, cheerful-looking face. She had dimples.

I tried to think of something witty to say, something that would win her over, inspire her to try a bit harder as soon as she realized I wasn't just any patient, how crucial it was that there be no complications.

"Ready," I said, but it came out feebly and then a mask was placed over my mouth and I was being told to count back from one hundred. I reached ninety-eight. I woke up eight hours later with a tube down my throat, a catheter uncomfortably lodged below, a splitting headache. At the nurse's direction, I coughed up the tube, dry-heaved. I was thirsty as

9

hell. My mother held a cup of ice that I ripped from her hand, wolfed down, and puked up into the kidney-shaped pan my father rested under my chin.

A stocky man in blue scrubs and a sweat-streaked surgical cap—Dr. Erwin Schachter, I would learn—bounded into my field of vision and proclaimed with a flourish that he had removed all of the mass he could see with his naked eye.

My mother's eyes were watery. My father was smiling; I saw the cleft in his square chin. It didn't occur to me that they were simply relieved I'd made it through the surgery. I was too bewildered. Naked eye? As opposed to what? Had he performed the operation without glasses?

But I was groggy and a sour dryness cottoned my mouth, and by the time I was done getting my lips to work and formulating a way to ask what he meant, the neurosurgeon was gone and my mother was laying her warm hand on my cheek and telling me I had gotten through it and now just to rest.

IV

Deinos. I passed the second buoy and I was gaining strength. Arms slicing through the water, legs churning, stroke in rhythm with my breathing, breathing in rhythm with my kick. Even the current seemed part of the sleek hydrodynamic engine that was my body, skimming me along the surface.

Deinos. The Ancient Greek word meaning both awful and awesome, terrible and wondrous.

Deinos as in dinosaur. Awful, terrible: the fear of hypothermia, of delirium, the fear of giving in to those fears and giving up. Awesome, wondrous: the extraordinary capacity of the mind to overcome, the body to recover itself, to regenerate, to heal.

Deinos. Out of nowhere the same word came into my

mind the day after my surgery. I stood before the bathroom mirror, regarding the wide-set hazel eyes, quiet and somber, like two standing pools in the middle of summer, then carefully peeled off the dressing to reveal the track of stitches scoring the right side of my scalp.

Deinos. Awful, terrible: my head cut open. Awesome, wondrous: my head sewn together again.

I felt like jumping up and down and throwing my arms in the air, but the bathroom floor was hard tile and I didn't want to risk a shock to my system. So I just clenched one fist and mouthed *Yeah, baby* to my reflection.

I said it soundlessly because there had been a subdued mood in the room that morning and I wasn't sure how to read it. Still, there was no denying what I was seeing. Apart from the stitches and my shaved head, I couldn't remember looking better—a little wan, perhaps, and yet oddly restored, the sleep-deprived look in my eyes gone, as if I'd just been to a spa.

Indeed, the only other remnant of the operation: a dull ache on the right side of my head that intermittently signaled its existence like a foghorn in the distance.

The hospital room was packed: a dozen people assembled around my bed, flowers and cards and boxes of chocolate covering every surface.

I sat propped on my pillows, basking in the doting attentions of the familiar faces that spoke to me slowly and softly and tenderly as if a loud noise might shatter my fragile self.

There was Jake, a former co-worker I'd dated on and off the past two years; after brushing a kiss near my stitches, he stationed himself like a sentinel in the back corner of the room, impassively observing the action. There was my friend Dotie, the pretty, free-spirited paralegal. She slipped me a few packs of condoms. "You never know," she whispered, winking at me. "Might get lucky."

There was my secretary with two other support staff

members from my law firm, all of whom tolerated my lol-lygagging whenever I needed to break the monotony of my work; they appeared at the foot of the bed and confessed with a guilty glee that they'd extended their lunch hour to visit me without authorization from the personnel manager.

"I may have to report you," I said to them, deadpan. "For the good of the firm." They laughed hard, stopped suddenly, lowered their eyes.

And all throughout, the phone was ringing. Sometimes I instantly recognized a caller; sometimes it took a while. The further back in my past, the easier to identify. I knew the nasal Yonkers squawk of my great aunt Adele but couldn't place the flat accent of someone who turned out to be an associate from my office.

That felt spooky, saying I was okay and cracking a few jokes to voices I didn't immediately recognize. But it was no good seeming muddle-headed. I needed to show everyone I was fine.

It was just what I told myself each time I strode into a meeting or conference or hearing. If I exuded self-assurance, I would be possessed by confidence. If I seemed fine, surely the rest would follow.

So I went on, even as my voice grew hoarse and reedy from overuse and the blunt throbbing pain in my head reasserted itself.

V

I swam on, tasting the salt in the water, at one with it. *Like a fish*, I said to myself, almost giddy.

Just then, my vision went blurry. My eyes stung. Salt water was leaking into my goggles. I squeezed my eyes shut. I didn't want to break my rhythm. The third buoy was an orange smear in the distance. I swam on.

At some point I lifted my head. The buoy was no closer—in fact, I seemed to have passed it.

All at once, I didn't feel so giddy. I looked behind— nothing but an expanse of choppy waves—then across. About fifty yards to my right, five or six fluorescent yellow heads bobbed amid a flurry of downward-arcing arms. I had missed the turn at the third buoy.

"Fucking fuck," I shouted into the wind. I yanked off my goggles and tightened the strap.

As I made for the other swimmers, exhilaration again surged through me: I could have panicked and I hadn't. A few strokes later, I felt the strap loosen. Salt water streamed into my eyes, blinding me. The goggles slipped down my face and drifted off, one end of the strap detached, useless. I flung them away. A wave broke into my face. A sea gull hooted from above.

That was when I felt myself relax. Here I was, alone in the Long Island Sound, way off course. I had no goggles, would likely be the last out of the water, but that was okay. I'd make it back. I knew that much.

Besides, things could be worse. Things could always be worse.

Picture this. You're lying on a conveyer belt that's slid- ing backward into the darkness of a narrow tunnel. Finally it stops. A ceiling hovers fewer than six inches over your nose. There's only a sliver of light at your feet.

You've never experienced anything like this. Until a few days ago, you've had only a passing acquaintance with dy- ing and death. You've never, in other words, had cause to fear dark, closed-in spaces.

That was me in the MRI machine in the late afternoon the day following my brain surgery. Those were my breaths coming broken and shallow. That was my hand thumping the sides, producing only a dull thud. And my voice calling out, tentatively at first, then ever more loudly, frantically, overwhelmed by the roar of the machine.

Eyes tightly shut, I began to count down from one hundred. If I could make it to zero, it would be over. But my mind wandered by ninety-three and I called out once again for relief, the words chafing my throat.

No answer. The machine had swallowed my voice.

My bladder felt full to bursting. I had to get out. Writhe, squirm, shimmy down toward the sliver of light.

"PLEASE DO NOT MOVE, DEAR," a voice boomed above the din. "YOU CANNOT MOVE."

The weight pressing on my bladder was unbearable. I heard short bursts like a fusillade. Then clicking. Clicking? What was happening? "Just let me out . . . please let me out . . . please, I have to go to the bathroom."

Someone pulled down my underpants, placed something under me. Nothing came. I began again. One hundred, ninety-nine . . .

If I could make it to zero, it would be over. I reached zero and it wasn't over. I began again from one hundred. And again.

"How are you feeling, Lisa?"

The voice was low and sweet-sounding, and betrayed a slight unidentifiable accent.

A doctor in a white coat set her chart on the bed table and lowered herself to eye level. She had porcelain skin and eyes the color of soft charcoal. "I am Dr. Afshari," she said with a certain solemnity. "One of the staff psychiatrists. You had an MRI and have been in some distress?"

I swiveled up to a sitting position, smacked my lips together, and began to speak. Cruel. I kept using the word cruel to describe the tidal wave of panic that had shaken me to my very core. I didn't care if I was making sense. I just needed to let go of the memory of being trapped in darkness, the feeling that whatever I did, I couldn't escape, whatever I did, I had to

14

stay in the darkness.

"Why don't you tell me about your family." She produced a small pad and a pen from her jacket.

I blinked. "Am I making any sense?" I asked.

"You're fine," she said. "Tell me about your family."

So I told her about my father, a professor of international law, my mother, the chief social worker at a school for troubled adolescents in New Haven. I told her they divorced when I was eleven, that the divorce was a bitter one, and my stepmother Christiane, who emigrated from Iran, was an international lawyer at the United Nations.

"Oh," she said with a small smile, tucking a wisp of ink-black hair behind her ear. "I am Iranian too." I liked that she told me something about herself. It humanized things. And that she was taking notes, as if what I was saying mattered.

"Actually, we're not close." I pushed myself up straighter. "We've never been." I blamed her for breaking up our family, I said, and we had never really recovered from that.

"Sisters? Brothers?"

"There's Luke. Dutch for cutie pie, or something like that. My father had a Fulbright in The Hague, that's how she got it." Her real name was Anna, I added, and she was married in June, and she and her husband Cary were doctors at Johns Hopkins in Baltimore.

"So she is older than you?" Dr. Afshari's pen was suspended above the pad. She had fleshy fingers.

"Yeah, less than two years." I rolled my eyes in the direction of the ceiling, straining to calculate the age difference. I needed to get it right. I needed to show her my mind still worked. "Eighteen months."

Dr. Afshari asked if I had other siblings. "My younger sister Debbie," I said. "We call her Pip. She's mentally retarded and profoundly autistic and mute, never uttered a word, and she's the reason my parents never speak." I told her about the ten years she had consumed my mother's life, long after it was clear there was no hope that she would talk, much less require anything less than full-time care. "So finally my mom insisted on sending her to a residential school so she could at least learn some basic life skills, and my father saw it as her abandoning Pip, and he's never forgiven her. Ever. To this day."

"How old is Pip now?"

"Thirty," I said. "So . . . seventeen months—I'm seventeen months older. And then there's my half-sister Marjy. She's six."

I told her of my abortive run at a Ph.D. in Ancient Greek and Latin in the years after college, of my recent resignation from my law firm, of my plan to buy a car and travel around the country until I figured out what to do next.

"And now this," I said. "No warning, nothing. They haven't said anything for sure, but I think they may have gotten it all. I mean, I just don't see how . . ." Did she nod ever so tinily? How I wanted her to nod. How I wanted her to say they'd gotten it all.

I talked and talked about myself and my family. I can't say what else I told her, only that by the end, I felt purged, purified, renewed. Her dark eyes, riveted on me, reflected an ineffable empathy, a wisdom too old for the smoothness of her skin.

"So I will be back, okay?" she asked, no-nonsense, as she rose and headed out the door.

"Please." I tried to to arrange my features into a smile.

"Fifteen laps to a mile," bassooned an orderly in blue scrubs about five minutes later.

"Let's do three," I said to Luke, still invigorated from my talk with Dr. Afshari. Less than a quarter of a mile but it was a start.

From the rooms opening off the corridor came a medley of sounds: the hearty exchange of greetings, hushed murmurs, Arlo Guthrie's adenoidal twang from a radio, antiseptic quiet.

16

I made it my business not to look into any room, not so much out of any respect for privacy as to preserve the fiction that I was not a patient like them; that all this was not happening to me; that I, unlike them, could amble through the halls, as if warming up for a run in the park.

In truth, what I feared was the sight of someone in the same plight as me but in even worse shape, someone spouting inanities, drooling from one side of her mouth, one useless eye drooping in its socket, all the while waving at me to come in for a visit.

Luke and I continued on our way, doing imitations of Mrs. Gorman, the formidable, chain-smoking teacher we both had for fourth grade.

"Still the troublemaker, Miss Reisman," my sister said, her Mrs. Gorman-voice gravelly.

"Afraid so, my dear girl," I rasped, looking over at her. Her eyes behind her glasses were pretty, almond-shaped, but with a certain opacity, like looking into a screened-in porch. "But isn't this fun."

VI

I was back on course, back in rhythm, my stroke smooth and economical, my breathing easy, my body gliding along. Without the goggles, I had to keep my head above the water, but even that was okay; when my neck got tired, I dipped my face in for a moment or two.

The water was calm, temperate. Everything seemed calm and temperate. The shore was in view but I didn't want to get out, wasn't ready to face the handful of tepidly cheering onlookers, to brave the rain-slicked roads.

We waited on vinyl chairs in an L-shaped alcove. Luke and Cary faced my mother and me. My father, maintaining his estrangement from my mother, sat perpendicular to us against

17

the wall, his oversized briefcase resting on the empty chair beside him.

We hid our tension behind a façade of small talk and tired jokes. I overheard someone on the pay phone behind us rejoicing that his tumor was benign and making plans to have a celebratory dinner at a Thai restaurant in the Village. I wanted my Walkman so I could tune him out.

I stared at my left sandal. Luke must have gone up to my apartment to get some of my clothes. At some point. How little I knew about what had gone on outside myself the week I was at the hospital. And where I would go after the meeting with Dr. Schachter—how had I not thought to ask? And, above all, what had been taken out, much less what it might mean. I had been too preoccupied with holding myself together.

What I knew about the tumor had reached me incidentally and in fragments and was confusing if not contradictory: a mention by a doctor to Luke and my father the day after the surgery of "problematic" cells in the center; another remark, more recent, by Luke, that it was likely of a lower grade—1 or 2, as opposed to the highest, 4—and would require radiation treatments at most. No one, it seemed, knew anything for sure.

The only certainties were that the diagnosis would come from the report of the pathologist who examined the tumor—I pictured a lizardly guy somewhere in the bowels of the hospital lifting it out of a tall pickle jar with a pair of tongs. And that presently we would get the results of the report from Dr. Schachter.

"Rize-man Rice-man?" A small dark-eyed woman appeared in the alcove, reading our name from a clipboard and peering around.

I felt a stinging around my stitches. My hand went to my baseball cap to still the sensation.

"Do you mean Reisman?" my father asked, hardening the -e-. He stood up. The jacket of his gray suit was creased and his usually symmetric knot of his tie was askew. "Lisa Reisman?"

She held the clipboard closer to her face. "Right," she said, nodding. "Lisa Reisman."

My mother sat ramrod straight. My father's knees jittered and twitched. Luke shifted positions every few moments. Cary stared at the clock, checked his watch, adjusted his glasses. I waited motionless, perched in a sort of highchair, barely breathing.

Finally Dr. Schachter hurried in, doughy in washed-out blue scrubs and a mop of gray hair. He nodded at us soberly and installed himself on a green leather stool with wheels. The stinging around the stitches had settled into a dull, pulsating throb.

A nurse entered the room, holding an oversized manila envelope. "Ah," he said, reading the top of the envelope. "Rizeman." He had no idea who I was.

"Reisman. You took a tumor out of my brain last week?"

"Right," he said, evidently still trying to place me. He slid the scan from the folder and inspected it. "So, you'll be doing your radiation treatments here, I take it," he said, not looking up.

Quietly I exulted—that I needed only radiation, that it was not so serious as to require chemotherapy.

"We thought she'd go to Yale—both my parents live close by," Luke was saying. "We've already talked to a few oncologists up there."

"Who." It wasn't a question. He was still inspecting the MRI.

Luke named the doctors.

"Very good," he said. "All fine doctors." His beeper, clipped to the waist of his pants, interjected. He eyeballed its message and sighed. "Just one moment."

A moment later he was back, restationing himself on his stool. "So, where were we?"

Silence. I closed my eyes. The clock ticked. I felt a wave of heat, then a lightness, as if I'd floated out of my chair and was watching the proceedings from somewhere above. "What did the pathologist find," I heard myself saying, the words clear, distinct, my voice oddly calm, the only question there was.

"Ah, yes," he said. "Wait one more moment. I think the report is being printed out just now." He left again.

"Yes, now I remember," he said on his return, waving a piece of paper. "It's glioblastoma. Multiforme. Grade 4." He spoke casually, almost offhandedly, and for a moment I tried in vain to recall what Luke had said about the grade—was higher better, like a higher test score?—but only for a moment. "I'm sorry," he was saying.

I think I asked what this meant and I might have stammered out a few more questions but already my heart was sinking like a stone through deep, dark water. My eyes glistened. I felt them pooling with tears and I blinked rapidly, trying to maintain my composure.

Scraps of conversation swirled about.

"Highest grade"

"most aggressive form"

"radiation?"

"won't be enough"

"even if you thought you got everything?"

"doesn't matter"

"if the chemotherapy doesn't?"

"some promising clinical trials"

"survival rate?"

"not necessarily a death sentence, no, absolutely not, not at all"

"yes yes, palliative, if it comes to that"

My father was feverishly taking notes on a small pad. Luke's face was frozen. At some point everyone stood up. As I rose, I felt my cheeks burning and my heart kicked as if I'd been shot, like a bird in flight.

I must have thanked the surgeon and made my way, unseeing, through the waiting room, out of the hospital, and into the blinding sun.

BIKE

I

Rocks and pebbles on the sandy shore cut into the soles of my feet. The two or three remaining spectators clapped, a forlorn sound on a wet, gray morning. Legs rubbery, I waved and made for the transition area.

Every moment counts in a triathlon, but my bike was nowhere to be found among the empty racks on the green expanse, and when I finally tracked it down at the far end of the farthest rack from the entrance, my teeth were chattering and my toes were numb. I wiped my feet clean with a soggy towel, my hands as stiff as boxing gloves, then dug into my waterproof bag for my shorts and T-shirt. The shirt was solid green. No silk-screened slogan. Nothing to mark the ten years and one month since my diagnosis.

There had been a party for my fifth anniversary at a Soho bistro, a loose agglomeration of friends from my former law firm and a few from the graduate program I'd just finished, lifting their glasses to toast my health. And the same for my seventh, after I'd moved from the city to my mother's shoreline town in Connecticut.

But there would be no celebration for my tenth. It seemed tired. And presumptuous. How many times, as the years wore on, could I revel in defying mortality? And wasn't that what birthdays became after a certain age, even if dressed up in cakes and singing and tired AARP jokes?

Besides, the so-called anniversary date is bogus, really. Once you're confronted with a deadly illness, either the treatments work or they don't. Either you live or you die. And when the treatments end, you don't get a medal or a plaque. You get a good-bye, a good luck, and a follow-up appointment.

That's when the clock should start ticking. You've just been in an all-consuming battle for your very existence. It's not simply what's next. It's relearning how to live. And figuring out how to make yourself worthy of your survival.

At that I'd come up short.

Which was why I needed to do something that would breathe life into every fiber of my being. Not ziplining over the Rocky Mountains or parachuting into the Grand Canyon or running with the bulls. That wasn't my style.

No, I wanted to push my body to the limit. I wanted my brain to push my body to the limit. I wanted pain. I wanted suffering. I wanted to prove that I was not just well but at the apex of fitness. I wanted to rejoice in that.

As I was strapping on my helmet, I heard my name. My mother and her best friend Myra were charging through the parking lot in bright slickers. My mother was waving a Ziploc bag. "Lise!" she shouted. "Lisa! Protein bars!"

I mounted my bike and threaded my way out of the transition area toward them. I felt sheepish, being one of the last competitors. I was supposed to be the athlete of the family, after all.

Then again, neither of them cared. They just wanted to make sure I got something in my system. My mother, especially. She'd been dubious about the triathlon—until I got deep into my training and she saw there was no turning me back. She'd stepped aside but still she worried. "Could she have a seizure doing this?" I overheard her asking Luke on the phone earlier that week. And the night before, her insistence on protein bars. Ten years later.

No one goes through the crisis of a serious illness alone; I'd learned that much. There's collateral damage, and it doesn't end with the treatments.

Which was another reason I was doing the race. As a material way to show my mother—to show everyone, but in particular my mother—how, without her, I would never have been in such peak condition, let alone above-ground. So it could be her celebration too.

"Got 'em," I called out to them as I turned onto the road, feeling the aching heaviness in my arms. The swim had taken its toll.

I reached into my pocket, tore open the wrapping of a protein bar with my teeth, and with the intense admixture of nuts and sugar charging through me, I set off, my tires hissing on the slippery road.

If I exerted myself at all during the steamy mid-August week after my discharge, it was from room to room of my step-mother's Upper East Side apartment. I would stay there for six days with Luke and Cary before they drove me to my mother's house in Connecticut to start my radiation and chemotherapy treatments.

In spite of my inactivity, I was ravenous. For meat. Red meat. And I had been a vegetarian since college.

Most days I was awakened before dawn by fierce cravings for Big Macs and chili dogs and Slim Jims. As Cary and Luke slept in the guest room, my father, already up and preparing for an international arbitration, resolutely pounded the pavements of Lexington Avenue in earnest search.

The second morning I waited for what seemed like hours, stomach yowling with hunger. He returned with a sesame roll wrapped in plastic. Upon inspecting its contents— thick slab of pink meat marbled in fat and gristle—I reassembled the sandwich and polished it off.

It was the steroid Decadron that was stirring my lust for sausage biscuits and fried pork rinds and meatball grinders, its price for decreasing the swelling in my brain. I was taking it four times a day, along with its trio of antidotes: Zantac to prevent stomach ulcers, Bactrim to ward off pneumonia, and Compazine for nausea. There was also Dilantin to thwart further seizures and Percocet for the lingering headaches. Not to mention stool-softening Colace and Senna to unblock the whole works.

The latter two didn't do what they were supposed to do for almost a week. That was the worst, contemplating all those saturated fats, all those prescription drugs, putrescing in my system.

Among the medications waging their separate campaigns, I drifted, shell-shocked and spaced out, dislocated in thought and emotion, oriented only by the phone calls through the day. I don't recall with whom I spoke or much of what I said, just the strange sense that great meaning was being derived from my illness, that I was being used to put everyone else's troubles into perspective.

Sometimes, when the outlay of pity was a bit too thick or someone had wrung from me the most horrid details of my ordeal, I'd hang up the phone in gagging disgust.

For the most part, though, I relished the calls. I was being eulogized and I was still alive.

And then there was Bob. Luke had enlisted me in a buddy program run by the hospital. The program would pair me with a long-term cancer survivor who had been confronted with a diagnosis similar to my own. Before we left the hospital, Luke was told that my buddy's name was Bob and that he would be in touch.

I awaited Bob's call with great eagerness, awaited the opportunity to talk with someone on the inside, someone who could tell me that the terror I was refusing to feel was normal and that maybe I had a chance. When Bob didn't contact me for five days, I grew concerned that he had died. I suspected my sister was thinking the same thing, but she didn't let on.

I should have known right away by his voice—nasal, phlegmy, the kind of voice that makes you want to somehow clear his throat for him. I should have known when, less than five minutes into our conversation, Bob declared that he had lost all his pubic hair as a result of the chemotherapy. And when Bob told me that after one of his treatments he had clean forgotten how to spell the word "soap" and had to hunt down the word in the dictionary and then drew a blank on where to look after the letter –s–, I should have escaped then and there.

But I stayed on, riveted in horror, my hand clutching the phone so tightly that the sweat made the receiver slip through my fingers and clatter onto the hardwood floor. As I lifted it back to my ear, I heard Bob's voice—he had not realized the phone had dropped—rambling on about his lazy right eye, yet another side effect of his surgery.

Soon after Bob made me promise that I would attend his brain tumor support group, the torture ended. I had no intention of going but my bowels were rumbling. Bob had singlehandedly done what the Colace and Senna could not.

He had, quite literally, scared the shit out of me.

II

I was flying. I was picking off cyclists one by one, making up the time lost in the turbulent swim. Past a wide-set cyclist, her meaty calf marked 39 to signal her age, my wheels whisking along the wet road; past a lanky guy in a Speedo—a Speedo? was he European? and on a slim racing saddle?—laboring over a hill—I couldn't catch his age; past the four-mile marker; past a sixty-three-year-old woman, the back of her singlet reading CAN'T STOP GRANNY. In the foggy distance, I made out a bright yellow helmet. Tucking my head down, I shifted to a higher gear and began my pursuit.

I was breathing hard, breathing in the metallic scent of rain, the sulfurous marshlands, but I felt nothing. I was in a cadence, a cadence with the road. There's a reason the word endorphin comes in part from morphine.

This was what I loved about cycling. The freedom of it. No cares. No one beginning a conversation with *how are you feeling?* five, six, even seven years after my treatments—the surest indication that, no matter what I did, I would be perceived as someone ill, chronically ill, someone still in recovery, someone—that loaded, loathsome phrase—in remission. It could come back.

No, this was just me and my mind and my body and the open road, the wind zipping by, the raindrops pattering my arms, just my legs propelling me forward, forward, forward.

As I crested another hill, I heard it approaching from behind: the whir of wheels, a *hegh-hegh-hegh*, the click of gears.

I looked back. And saw the line of cyclists I had passed gaining on me. It's an impulse, looking back, assessing your position. It's an impulse that must be fought, my high-school cross-country coach used to tell us. Fogs your clarity of focus. Lets your opponents know you're weakening. Ushers in the specter of defeat.

The coach, who had a handlebar moustache and indecipherable tattoos stenciled up and down his wiry arms, was an autodidact, with a fondness for dropping words like specter and autodidact. When I learned the word for "small manual"—*enchiridion*—in my college Ancient Greek class, I thought of him. Not because he would have used it on his disciples: too abstruse, he would have said. Because he had given me a little handbook on life.

That didn't stop me from looking back, though. And that was a mistake.

Ten years before, I couldn't help myself either. From the back window of the rental car I was scanning the New York cityscape for the distinctive mirrored skyscraper housing my former law firm as Cary pulled onto the FDR Drive. It had been six days since my discharge and the first time I had ventured outside.

"There it is," I called up to the front seat before heeding Luke's order to lie back down. "Farewell, billable hour, farewell, slippery corporate ladder, farewell, sleazeball opposing counsel. Farewell to all."

"Harsh," said Luke as she directed Cary toward the New

England Thruway for the ninety-minute drive to my mother's house in Connecticut. "You remember how much you loved it at the beginning?"

"Sure I do." My head resting on the leather seat, I watched the clouds scudding across the August sky and inhaled the familiar rank odor of the East River. "I loved all of it." Loved the impregnable black-letter propositions pieced together from the most quotidian and petty disputes, the muscular turns of phrase—*overwhelming weight of authority, incontrovertible evidence, wholly implausible interpretation.* Savored the process of honing legal papers that expertly sank the blade into any flank of the enemy posing a threat to our position, that systematically crippled and lamed the other side with a calculated series of assaults and offensives until it was left with no option but to surrender.

In the beginning, *Good job, Reisman,* scrawled in red ink atop my work by Cal Hirsch, Esq., the well-heeled chief of the labor and employment department, had been all I needed to fuel me through the wee hours of the morning. And the office thirty-three floors above midtown Manhattan, the secretary, the expense account, the Lincoln town car whisking me home, the parties at the "21" Club and the Four Seasons—none of those hurt. My life assumed the relevance I had daydreamed about as I drifted through a Master's in Ancient Greek and Latin, a starched and predictable order, a sheen that blinded me to any concern but recognition and success.

Until it dawned on me, in the latter part of my first year as an attorney, that researching and writing, drafting and revising were all I was doing. Until I noticed that Hirsch was parading my fellow associates before company vice presidents and circuit court judges while I remained behind, stashed away in my office or in the library behind stacks of *Federal Reporters* and bulging accordion files.

It was Jake who suggested I pay Cal Hirsch a visit in his corner office about fourteen months into my legal career. Jake

Weyerhauser, the head of IT, had been hired about a year after me. I liked him immediately, his twinkly eyes, his lean soccer-player physique, the way he grinned irreverently at me, Scotch in hand, at the monthly firm cocktail party.

We sent inane phone messages to each other through our secretaries and flirted in the law firm library. He had a girl-friend but they were on the rocks and I hadn't dated anyone seriously since law school and we were always at the office, so it was only a matter of weeks before I was tasting the pepper-mint chapstick on his lips under the concrete overhang just outside our building late one autumn evening, and from there it was an easy step to his apartment, which was within walking distance of the firm.

"Why not just tell the guy you want more experience on the outside?" Jake asked when he caught me staring at the plastered swirl on the ceiling of his studio in the dim light of morning. The day before, Hirsch had pointedly averted his gaze as we crossed paths in the hall.

Cal Hirsch was not a tall man, maybe a few inches un-der six feet, but he was built like a Neanderthal and carried himself as such. He had a dull glaze in his eyes suggestive of an unfed mastiff and a temper to match. Associates quaked before him. I was no exception.

"Time, Reisman," he snorted, sausage fingers hitched through the button loops of his blood-red suspenders, when I earnestly told him I wouldn't mind observing an oral argu-ment, maybe, or sitting in on a strategy session with clients. "Give it time."

He used declarative sentences only with his fellow part-ners and the high-ranking company officials he represented, but otherwise spoke in short, nasal bursts. I didn't mention how I dreamed of being in the thick of the action, holding forth before a rapt jury, the sheer eloquence of my words swaying them to our side. I calculated it would be better to prove my worth in stages.

The time never came—which is not to say I was never let out. Beryl Barry was a junior partner whose diminutive stature belied her fierce ambition to distance herself from her Bedford-Stuyvesant working-class background and steeled her take-no-prisoners attitude to anyone who blocked her path. Perhaps it was her intense dislike of Hirsch that prompted her to assign me more and more work. Or maybe she saw in me something that her senior colleague couldn't.

I never knew. Beryl Barry was not one for small talk. Whatever the case, she let me hand her exhibits at depositions and trials, once even gave me an arbitration to defend a wrongful discharge claim.

But the elation that followed my resounding triumph at that arbitration proved short-lived—as did the hope that my strong performance would prompt some change in Hirsch. Less than a week later, I heard him summoning associates to a client seminar. I sat rigid in my swivel chair, staring blankly at my dulled reflection in the computer screen, stung with envy. My office felt like a small box.

I got up, walked to the vending machines, and stood for a long while in front of the barbecued chips and moon pies and Sun Chips, scouring my memory for something I had said or done that had incurred Hirsch's evident lack of confidence in anything other than my written work. I found nothing. My dollar got stuck in the machine.

Sure, I made that comment to the senior associate Hirsch was grooming for partner that he looked like he'd eaten a lot of meatloaf as a youth. And there was the time I saw Hirsch's raised eyebrows when he spotted me with a friend from corporate going round and round in the revolving doors without leaving or entering the building. He must have heard when I'd been sent home on "Casual Friday" for wearing a pair of jeans with a hole in the knee and again the next week, despite the fact that I had neatly patched up the hole, must have been told about my juggling demonstration for the receptionist.

But those were minor transgressions, a way to blow off steam in the staid preserve of a white-shoe Manhattan law firm, wholly unrelated to my capacity to advocate for his clients. If anything, it showcased that streak of singularity that would distinguish me from my peers, the same streak that Beryl Barry likely recognized and appreciated.

When I got home that night, I turned out the lights and lay down on my futon, listening to myself breathe. My phone rang. I let the answering machine click on. It was Jake, wondering why my office was dark; I almost never left before eleven. I stayed on the futon. My eyes were tearing and my head hurt and I felt too gutted of spirit to call him back.

I set my alarm for 7:30 a.m., an hour later than usual. That would become a ritual, as would my memorization of poetry on the walk to the subway station. I don't know why I lit upon "The Love Song of J. Alfred Prufrock" and I never quite grasped its meaning, but the idea of measuring my life in coffee spoons and seeing the moment of my greatness flicker must have resonated with the gathering sense of desperation that awaited me in the office day after day.

I began to feel it all. The small, hard angry corns and calluses that rubbed and chafed in the close confines of my medium-heeled pumps. The stockings, as oppressive as the physical environment of stale air and sealed windows. The pin-striped business suits, my surrender to the faceless ranks of associates. The sycophantic expression I plastered on my face each day, the look that declared my eagerness to please, my zeal to help in any way I could. The pressure to speak and act and look a certain way, to talk the platitudinous talk of weather, sports, and weekend plans.

Soon I was wearing more comfortable mules instead of pumps and substituting pants suits for skirts, one lilac pants suit in particular, which I sported at least twice a week. I turned down assignments I once would have longed for, pleading *swamped, drowning, couldn't give it the time it de-*

serves, while accepting work only from Beryl Barry. To break the sense that the walls of my office were closing in on me, I took long lunches and longer walks.

My one-bedroom underwent a complete renovation: my bookcase categorized and alphabetized; my stereo un-boxed and set up; my CDs dusted off and classified by genre. Maybe I was trying to make a life for myself in my apartment. Maybe I believed that the process of restoring order, however cosmetic, would lay bare a way to rediscover my lost enthusiasm. I spent one night listening to Johnny Cash's A*t Folsom Prison* to jar myself from my malaise with its toe-tapping boom-chicka-boom two-beat, but it only left me envying the prisoners: at least they had order and definition in their lives. Another night I stumbled through passages of *The Iliad* and *The Odyssey* with my Homeric lexicon, recalling the dictum of a Classics professor of mine that those were the only two books one ever needs to read.

Just as my disenchantment was sliding into terminal in-difference, a senior partner retired. Beryl Barry replaced him. She called me into her office. This was early September, a time of new beginnings—and, as it turned out, a time to harvest opportunity.

"Reisman," she said in her gruff Brooklyn accent, her iron-gray, power-hungry eyes boring into my hazel-browns. Her tiny fist came down on her oceanic desk. "Help me take him down." The identity of *him* was understood.

I represented a client at an arbitration hearing; there was fear, then exhilaration. I did a second; there were less of both. I argued motions, against turning over certain documents to the other side, to compel a witness to appear at a deposition. I counseled clients on how to discipline a chronically late employee, on the grievance procedures in a sexual harassment policy. My pumps didn't hurt my feet as much and my stockings didn't seem so stifling.

And then, seven or eight months later, they did. As did

that needling sense of pointlessness and the urge to escape. Even when I couldn't fight it, even as I dawdled at a diner with my hard-backed copy of *Bleak House* and a half-eaten grilled cheese sandwich, I didn't feel free, just empty and useless, just lonely.

And angry. Angry at the old man for smacking his lips together in the booth next to mine, angry at Jake for not calling me for weeks, for not getting what I was going through, though there was no way he could have been aware of it; earlier that spring, I told him I needed space for a while and he said sure, to take as long as I needed, which only left me feeling guilty and then angry at him for making me feel guilty. And, above all, angry that no one at the firm, including Beryl Barry, seemed to have noticed how much I was gone.

I would learn later that Beryl Barry was engaged in a bitter custody battle with her ex-husband over their two young children. Had I know it then, I doubt it would have moved me to sympathy. I was too deep in my gloom, too hungry for a sharp reprimand, something that would startle me from my doldrums, that would signal that I was valued and missed. Or maybe I had just stopped caring.

I don't remember anyone—my father; my mother; Luke—trying to talk me out of quitting my job—probably because whatever they might have said I wouldn't have heard. And though I can still see the lipstick-red convertible with the FOR SALE sign in its window parked on my street one morning that spring, I can't say how that led to my plan to motor around the country until I figured out what to do next.

Nor do I recall any reaction on the mid-June day—my thirty-second birthday—that I announced my resignation, only Beryl Barry's insistence that I attend the pre-trial settlement conference scheduled for the first week of August on a case she had assigned to me at the beginning of her reign as senior partner. It had been dormant for months.

By then, I was spending my hours in the office at my desk, fingers twined behind my head, contemplating the spongy ceiling tiles. Or adding to my rubber-band ball. Or rotating toward the window, watching people scurry about below, coveting their seemingly purposeful, untroubled lives. Or stepping out of my office to chat with my secretary or a member of the support staff or whichever associate happened to be around. "I'm just going to spit out the butt-ends of my days and ways," I'd tell them, loosely quoting "Prufrock." "Spit 'em out, get behind the wheel and eat up the space, drink it in." "Get lost," I'd say. "Get lost until I find my way."

It felt good to talk like that, almost as if I were already there, already gone; it made me feel powerful, like some free-spirited adventurer. From time to time, I took a call from a client or absently attended a meeting or idly paged through the case file in preparation for the settlement conference—until it struck me sometime during the afternoon of Friday, July 31 that I had no idea what position I would take and what arguments I would deploy to support it. But mostly I worked on my rubber-band ball which, I noticed, had neared softball proportions, as I took one last glance at the case file, shut off the lights in my office, and headed for the gathering at the bar.

But on Monday, August 3, my office remained dark. And on Friday, August 7, I wasn't taking permanent leave of the firm; I was languishing on a hospital bed, leading Dr. Af-shari on a tour of the low-hanging branches of my family tree. In the third week of August, I wasn't hitting the open road; I hadn't set foot on a used-car lot—I wasn't even allowed to drive, not for six months from the date of my seizure. At a time when I had intended to strike out into the world, alone and autonomous, driven by a fierce determination to find my true calling, I was sprawled in the back seat of a car, a post-op passenger being delivered to my mother's house for an indefinite stay.

Not to say I was particularly disheartened about it.

Truth was, notwithstanding my bold designs, which I'd blithely share with anyone who would listen, I'd been scared silly about leaving the law. Night after night during my last month of work, I lay awake, twisting and turning, besieged by doubt, agonizing over the undoing of my well-appointed life, any opportunity for rest drowned out by a jangling disquietude that I could not turn back.

"You okay back there, Lise?" my sister asked. She peered into the rearview mirror, her sunglasses reflecting the red construction cranes overlooking New Haven Harbor. ABBA was belting out "Waterloo" on the radio.

"Fine," I said, straightening up as it hit me, the vastness of the unknown. It was no longer where I would live or who might visit me. I had nothing to return to. Or did I? Would the firm make some sort of special exception, given my circumstances, let me work from home, or offer an open invitation to come back when I could? Then again, there was no escaping the fact that I had resigned.

"Almost there, Lise," Luke was saying. I barely heard her. I was trying to remember why I had quit. Was it that I no longer wanted that life? Or that Hirsch had early on perceived what I couldn't, that I had neither appetite nor flair for button-holing clients, quailed at the prospect of haggling with opposing counsel, and during oral arguments chronically faltered in my attempts to sway a judge to our side? Was it my incurable impulse to stir up trouble that explained my odd behavior—or some sense that I had less at stake because I wasn't long for that particular world? Did that sense of my own limitations— that I could never be much more than a brief-drafting desk jockey—explain my increasing apathy?

"Exit 53," Luke was telling Cary. I stared out the window at an orange sticker on the windshield of a brown sedan abandoned on the shoulder. *Get lost until I find my way?* It sounded impressive, but had it occurred to me what I would do if my car broke down or the top of the convertible got jammed open on a chilly night in the Badlands of South Dakota? *Eat up the space, drink it in?* Well and good, but I don't remember considering just how long I might subsist on a convenience-store diet of microwaved bean burritos and Mountain Dew before my body went into some sort of revolt. Or whether I had the self-sufficiency to withstand entire days on seven-word conversations with gas-station attendants. Or where I would sleep and how safe it would be and, even assuming I would feel safe, whether I'd have the grit to keep going, no matter how lost or lonely or discouraged I'd become.

Eventually, I would reflect on whether it all had been just talk. Just not on that soft mid-August afternoon. Not when the tires scraped onto the gravel driveway behind my mother's familiar white Honda and I saw her picking her way down the front steps, her arms widening, a smile brightening the worry that shrouded her features. Not when I settled into her embrace and felt the muscles in my jaw, my neck, my shoulders loosen, felt how knotted they had been. Nor when I sank into the patchwork chair while Luke and Cary brought in the bags, the chair in which she had nursed Luke and me, in which in junior high I used to lace up my sneakers for an afternoon run, in which for a moment I could linger and imagine myself healthy and strong and carefree.

III

Gradually, a pattern was developing. First, CAN'T STOP GRANNY, whom I'd passed about two miles before, overtook me. In close pursuit was Speedo guy and, not long afterward, the thirty-nine-year-old wide-set woman. I was pedaling my mountain bike twice as fast as each of them and yet each was gliding by me as though I were riding in slow motion.

That's how it felt in the months after the end of my treatments. An urgency to move on, move past what had happened, to re-invent myself. Reinvent. I used that word a lot those days. I could do whatever I wanted; I said that too.

It never occurred to me that my treatments didn't end my recovery at all, that my illness, at least figuratively, was still in my head. Nor that I had the luxury to be lost. I had health insurance, savings, a place to live.

All I knew was that I had to keep moving forward. Staying in place meant I was inert, lethargic, sick.

Better yet, I wasn't so lost. Which was why the idea of a road trip never re-entered my mind. There wasn't time. More than that, I no longer had to go searching for my true calling.

Best of all, there was no such thing as a typical Yale Nursing School student, according to the amiably plump director when we met in her office two months after my last treatment. I had come to appreciate nurses over the course of my illness, I told her. I'd had enough of redistributing wealth among Fortunc 500 companies. I wanted to learn to do what they do, what they did for me. We smiled at each other. We bemoaned the shortage of nursing professors, discussed the increasing numbers of students pursuing nursing as a second career, application deadlines.

Twenty minutes later, I was trudging down the gleaming corridors of the nursing school. Sure, there was the heavy course load but I seemed highly motivated, the director accurately observed. And the prospect of sitting for two hours in a classroom at the local technical college every other weeknight to satisfy the prerequisites—I could manage that. It was the year of clinical work recommended before entering nursing school that gave me pause. Hadn't I earned a break from sick people for a little while?

Another cyclist passed, 73 on his leg. Seventy-three. A seventy-three-year-old? A wave of exhaustion washed over me. I dug around my soggy pockets for another energy bar, barbarically tore away the wrapper with my teeth, bit off an enormous chunk, and forced my legs to pump harder.

Sweat mixed with rain water streamed down my forehead, stinging my eyes. My wrists ached. My back had locked up. My feet, housed in my sodden running shoes, had yet to thaw from the swim. A pair of women on tricked-out racing bikes coasted by me, chatting away.

That was okay, though. This wasn't about fancy equipment. It was about getting to the finish line with what I had. It was about using the raw material in myself to get it done.

But already the two women were specks in the horizon.

When you're seriously ill, it's all about fancy equipment, about hitting up every connection you have to find the best doctors at the best hospitals offering the most cutting-edge treatments. Forget about going at it with a grass-roots, pound-the-pavement approach. There's no time. And forget about going it alone.

With one exception: the way you navigate the crisis that is your disease. That's all you. And all patients have their own way: immersing themselves in amateur oncology, perhaps, or joining a support group to commune with people in the same straits as they are, or finding strength in religion or spirituality.

For me, it was acquiring tunnel vision. The only way I could proceed was by keeping indistinct and undefined anything that might distract me from getting well.

That's where Luke and Cary came in, no more so than during the six days they stayed with me in the third week of August.

I still remember their final afternoon. I was camped out on the patchwork chair where, aside from my wobbly fifteen-minute loops around my mother's backyard and down to the small beach around the corner from her winterized cottage, I had been whiling away my waking hours dozing or leafing mindlessly through entertainment magazines.

As Cary clicked away at the computer in the study, my sister kneeled over the living room coffee table, color-pencil-ing what looked like a cauliflower on a large sheet of paper and asking me about headaches.

"Headaches," I repeated, shifting my position on the patchwork chair. Through the screen door wafted the faint odor of brine from Long Island Sound. Bob Marley was crooning softly on the stereo.

Headaches. Sometime in the last three weeks, I had lost the definition. Was a headache the sudden rush through the right side of my head that took the air out of me and left me so aghast that I was seizing or fainting that I'd freeze until my heart stopped slamming in my ribs? Or the pounding in my temple that had me inching my way down to the first floor that morning—eleven steps—the landing—a turn—two more to the hardwood living-room floor—hand gripping the wooden banister, eyes fastened on the next green-carpeted stair, for fear of losing my balance?

Maybe it was the way I'd be talking on the phone, begin a sentence, and by the middle forget where I was going—that had to be related to some problem in my head; then again, a problem wasn't necessarily an ache and I was no doubt preoccupied with sounding clear-minded. There was a dull throb of pain behind my eyes and some twinges on the right side of my head, but it could have been the strong mid-afternoon light filtering through the blinds.

"A bit better, I guess," I said, returning to *People.* Jennifer Aniston was in a "tattoo phase." It would be a while before I could make words out of how I felt. Besides, what was the use in re-enacting the drama in my head? Hadn't I caused enough drama?

That was when Cary emerged, bespectacled and rumpled, from the study, for a cup of coffee. The next morning, he and Luke would return to Baltimore, Cary to his medical research fellowship at Johns Hopkins, Luke to the East Baltimore inner-city clinic where she worked as a primary care physician. Both had long before run out of vacation days.

He had been at the computer most of the afternoon—most of that week, in fact. Looking back on those days with Luke and Cary, I can't recall when they weren't doing something—and not just researching treatments on the computer in the study. Arranging appropriate cocktails of medications at breakfast, mid-afternoon, and before I went to bed. Dialing up colleagues on the newest clinical trials for my disease. Heading off for McDonald's or Wendy's to meet my Decadron-induced cravings. Zeroing in on the best oncologists at Yale-New Haven Hospital, the ones that were taking no new patients, and somehow finessing me appointments.

But here's the oddest thing. What comes back to me most starkly is what they didn't do. They didn't tell me that there was no way of knowing the extent of damage to my brain, how much of my memory had been lost, and to what degree the tumor and the seizures and the surgery had slowed my synapses and otherwise impaired my cognitive function. Or that that within eight weeks the fuzz on my scalp would fall out as a result of the radiation treatments and there was a sixty percent likelihood it would never return.

They didn't mention how resistant glioblastoma cells are to conventional treatments, not least because most drugs can't cross the blood-brain barrier, a sort of physiological moat that guards the brain. Or, as a result of my explicit request to withhold my prognosis, that for my age and the grade of my tumor, I was likely to die in three months without any kind of treatment and, even with aggressive intervention, there was only a fifty percent chance I'd survive a year and a ten percent chance I'd still be around in two. Or that there was no documentation on anyone who had lived with the disease beyond five years.

I can't say exactly when I made up my mind to remain oblivious of how long, statistically, I had to live. Medical odds can't account for the unfathomable, of course. But that wasn't part of my reasoning. It was more a reflex toward self-preservation, same as my instinct against pressing Cary for more information about the two trials he had found that August afternoon in Connecticut.

In any event, neither seemed promising. One was still in the early stages—"a phase II," Cary said—so its side effects, as well as any damage it might cause long-term, weren't known. And the other would require a wafer to be surgically implanted into the tumor cavity.

Besides, my sister said, as she continued to fill in the right corner of her drawing, the general rule was to take the invasive route only when there was no other alternative.

"Fine with me, but what's the deal with the cauliflower?" I asked, lowering myself beside her. Moose, my mother's tawny long-haired cat, trotted in and stretched out in a square of sunlight near the casement windows. My mother was at orientation at her school.

"It's your cerebrum," she said. "For a visualization exercise." She picked up an eraser and vigorously rubbed away a corner of the red. At the front of the cerebrum, or brain, just behind the forehead, were my frontal lobes. She pointed to the area she had just rubbed out. "And that's your right frontal lobe," she told me. "Erased of disease. Free and clear." She blew away the pink bits and slid the paper toward me. "It's sort of crude, but you're supposed to stare at it at least three minutes a day, imagine your brain like that."

I said *hunh* and nodded but even then I knew there was little chance I'd do it—picturing my un-diseased brain would only remind me that it was in fact diseased and that seemed like a bleak daily exercise.

Still, watching her put the finishing touches on the drawing made me feel cared for, as did the sound of Cary's steps bounding up to the guest room one day that week—apparently, I had cried out during a two-hour nap I was taking each afternoon—not to mention the morsels of optimism he fed me as he sat cross-legged at the foot of my bed—good surgical results; youth; excellent below-the-neck health—and with such earnest doctorly conviction that for a time I believed I would be okay.

That's what Luke and Cary did those early weeks. They obstructed the medical implications of my condition and allowed me to believe there was still hope, to focus only on the next stair, the next step on the road.

But they saw what I was unwilling to see; they knew my prognosis; they knew about the impending hair loss and the possibility that my brain had suffered permanent damage; they knew the survival rate of this treatment and the risks of that protocol. And considering what they knew, either or both could have shown cracks in their demeanor but they never did. They never betrayed a thing.

Not that they could entirely shield me from what was happening and, more keenly, from what I had lost. Then again, neither could the most cutting-edge protocol. I was still bolting upright in the middle of the night, convinced that I had forgotten to call back a client or attend a meeting, still waking up each day with the work I had on my desk and what was on my calendar squarely on my mind, the pathway of those thoughts as well-trodden as my route from my apartment to the subway station every morning.

That its imprint faded each time I opened my eyes and saw one of my mother's ink drawings on the wall of her guest room and it again came to me that there were no clients to call or conferences to attend, no work to do at all; that the world I had known was over, leveled, and I had crossed into an entirely new one—there was no blindering me from that.

IV

"Go, mountain bike!" a scrawny guy in neon-orange

bike shorts and matching helmet called out as he speeded ahead just beyond the eight-mile marker.

Who was this sartorially challenged homunculus, passing me and worse, shouting encouragement as he did? How could he not recognize that the sheer act of overtaking another should be devastating, as if that person were knee-deep in mud?

That one came from my cross-country coach too. In the crucible of competition, anyone, whether it's someone gunning for the win or in the middle of the pack or just trying to press on, is that much more susceptible to setbacks. When you're pushing your body to the limit, it's your mind that's in charge. When you're telling yourself that your burning lungs are nothing, that your shaky legs will have plenty of time to recover once you've crossed the finish line, when you're trying to persuade yourself you're doing fine, that kind of setback is as demoralizing as surging ahead of another racer is revitalizing.

It was the feeling of powerlessness that I couldn't abide, still couldn't. Sure, I resembled a healthy person, had for the last nine years or so, but that didn't quiet the alarm that would sound any time a flicker of pain moved through the right side of my head or a dizzy spell unsteadied me or I sweated out another MRI every December. At least while I was being treated, I knew I was actively attacking the cancer. Afterwards I could do nothing except wait for it to come back.

Go, mountain bike! Now I understood. I was being gutsy, racing on a middle-aged thick-tired mountain bike, the same one I used to pedal along West End Avenue, across Seventy-second Street, and over to the Central Park loop, the same one I'd trained on throughout the summer on these very roads.

A long series of inclines was beginning. This was my opening. Genetically I was no sprinter. If I didn't build up a nice lead in a cross-country race, a more fleet-footed runner would outstrip me in the final stretch. Likewise I could spin my bicycle pedals only so fast. Years back I'd learned to compensate by crushing the opposition on the hills.

I took a swig from my water bottle, shifted to a higher gear, and prepared to blast my way to the top.

In the early weeks after my surgery, I wasn't thinking about surpassing anyone or where I was in relation to anyone else, or anything, for that matter, besides myself.

This is what happens when you're sick. Larger issues pale; the world shrinks. It's all about you, all about the next step—through the kitchen to the living room, around the backyard, and onto the route which Luke and I made it a ritual to walk after dinner.

Her last night in Connecticut, we made our way toward the water, sandals thocking on the asphalt. It was a soft late-summer dusk. The sea-salt wind drifted in from Long Island Sound, carrying with it the faint scent of barbecue. Here and there I stopped to rotate my shoulders and bend my torso from side to side. My back had been cramping; there was a persistent smarting sensation running between my shoulder blades and halfway down the left side of my spine that I attributed to the lumpy mattress in the guest room.

The headlights from a long line of cars beamed in our direction and for a moment, I imagined my own funeral procession, then felt safe beside my sister, felt a pang that she and Cary were leaving the next morning.

The last time I remembered feeling so close to Luke was the night my father called us down from our bedrooms to the living room for a family meeting. It must have been a month or so after my parents drove ten-year-old Pip to a school for autistic and mentally retarded children on Cape Cod.

Deborah Shai, or Pip, as she came to be called; no one remembers when. Born eighteen months after me, her first year she lay in a crib or was propped up in a chair or placed on the floor in an infant seat, meeting my funny faces and nonsense songs and tickling with a blank unfocused gaze, her only movements the seizures that intermittently jolted her small body.

Severe mental retardation, a doctor told my parents about eighteen months into her life. She'll never get better. Put her in an institution was the second opinion. My father punched a wall. It was the turning point in his life, he once said.

My parents, young, bright, and fiercely determined to prove the doctors wrong, immersed themselves in research, talked to experts, cast about for something—anything—to make their child right. When Pip was three, they learned about a controversial program for brain-injured children in Philadelphia. Its claim: if Pip were forced to follow the basic motor stages through which healthy babies progress, she would eventually catch up.

My father moved the mahogany dining room table into the garage and replaced it with a padded table. He assembled monkey bars for the so-called Brain Gym. He removed the kitchen door, installed brackets in place of the hinges, and locked a chin-up bar between the kitchen and dining room.

My mother drew up an elaborate chart to keep track of the regimen. Each time they patterned her on the padded table—repeatedly moving her head, arms, and legs to replicate the cross-patterned crawl of a baby—they'd put a check mark in a box, and Pip would be that much closer to getting around on her own, she explained to Luke and me one night at dinner, her dark hair pulled back from her long face, under the cozy lights of the kitchen.

Each time they set her tiny body in the halter under the monkey bars and guided her hands from rung to rung, Pip would be better able to hold a ball or a spoon, she told us. And each time they fitted her feet into stirrups attached to the chin-up bar and swung her body upside down, she was on her way to thinking better and, eventually, talking. (The more oxygen to the brain, the theory went, the better the potential for brain development.)

The more boxes they checked, she said, the closer Pip would be to a regular kid, and then everything would go back to the way it had been. A Bryn Mawr graduate in the midst of a Ph.D. program in comparative literature at Columbia, she remembers telling herself she'd return to her studies then.

Three years; twelve twenty-minute cycles through the Brain Gym each day; one cycle every hour. Every waking hour spent in the hope that Pip would improve to a normal level. Pip was taught to crawl, to walk, to walk up stairs, to run in a sort of flustered shamble.

When she was about six, the progress waned, then stalled. They had righted Pip's body, but not her glazed stare, the muted broadcast of the profound autism that would forever isolate her from us; not her propensity for screaming and crying fits, which she invariably unleashed if our family went out to Friendly's or Mr. Steak; not her practice of wandering off if my mother eased her attention for even one moment.

That my parents enrolled Pip in a day program in New Haven, which she would attend for the next four years, should have afforded at least part-time relief for my mother. It didn't. Pip was still a wordless sixty- or seventy-pound toddler without judgment or self-control; an accident waiting to happen; her early mornings and afternoons and evenings and weekends and holidays, and there was no end in sight.

At last she said enough. She was thirty-eight. Her ten-year-old daughter had never uttered a word. She showed no signs of discriminating anyone, much less her own mother, from a stranger. Pip needed to develop life skills, she maintained to my father. She'd have a far better chance at a residential school with professionals trained for just that purpose.

It wasn't about completing the Ph.D; that chance was long gone. Pip was a hole she was pouring her life into, she remembers telling him.

At the time he called us down to the living room for the family meeting, my father was a well-established figure at the law school. He was the youngest professor ever to be awarded tenure there. He had a legion of admiring students. He had published six books. My father was not on familiar terms with failure. To his mind, sending Pip away would constitute failure.

I took the steps two at a time, ending with a flying leap from the landing. In the month since my parents drove her away, I hadn't missed Pip at all. I was relieved she was gone.

And now it was only going to get better. Somehow I had it in my head that we were about to learn of a grand vacation my mother and father had planned, not the customary day trip to which Pip had limited us with her unpredictable behavior, but one that would last a week or even more, where we could hike and swim and sleep in a hotel room with a color television and do whatever we wanted.

I bopped around excitedly until my mother told me to please settle down. It was only then, as I joined Luke on the shag carpet, that I noticed the track lighting was dimmed and my mother and father looked too serious and sad for a holiday announcement.

Which of them said it I don't recall; most likely, it was a joint effort, one of their last. It doesn't matter, really; by the time they told us that the two of them needed to be apart for a while, that my father would be moving temporarily to an apartment in New Haven, a short walk from the law school, I was screaming, sobbing, raging.

I ran to the landing of the staircase and flung my arms around the banister. I was in the spring of my sixth-grade year but I cried the violent tears of a toddler who has tripped and fallen hard on something entirely unexpected.

I pleaded *no no please no*, wishing I could reverse my

dash down the stairs, to install myself back in my bedroom, doing whatever I had been doing, to keep everything the same as it had always been.

When I scan the whole expanse of my childhood, the prevailing image of my older sister is her closed oak-paneled bedroom door. I don't remember thinking I could confide in her, or ask her advice, or count on her to be on my side.

With one exception. On that terrible night, she got up from the rug and joined me on the landing, stroking my hair and telling me that everything was going to be alright.

That was my older sister. Stoic; sensible; composed. My mother always said she spaced our births so that we'd have each other as playmates and companions. It worked, except there was only room for one levelheaded sister and I had to come up with something else to be. When my father left and we found ourselves picking through the rubble that was our family, our qualities, once quaintly distinct, clashed.

The day after that living-room meeting, I remember climbing the stairs of my best friend Julie's house, my footsteps lost in the thick carpet. Every part of me ached.

Peals of laughter rang out from her bedroom, where she and one or two of my four other best friends were lounging on her bunk bed, gossiping. We were in our final weeks of elementary school, a close-knit clique that would take no new members, and I was the leader.

This was 1977, when one out of three marriages was breaking up in the United States, but among my clique and the rest of my classmates in our upper-middle-class enclave of New Haven, divorce was unheard of, at least to my ears. For my friends to see that my life, already blemished by a retarded sister, was even more imperfect, that the man of the house was leaving, was unimaginable. That marked one of the last afternoons I would spend at Julie's.

Luke, in contrast, seemed barely touched. When school

began the next fall, she didn't skip lunch, hiding out in a carrel in the library, for fear of being seen sitting alone. She joined her bevy of friends in the cafeteria. The A's still ran down her report card like the tracks of a one-legged bird.

I don't recall how it was that I found myself following Luke and my father toward the corner of Third Avenue and Forty-sixth Street that same autumn. But I can still see the shadows shifting such that the woman waiting for us at first sight resembled my mother, a younger, more polished incarnation of her, but with the same dark-featured look, the same elegant carriage.

And when I saw that she wasn't, when my father introduced the woman who would become my stepmother to Luke and me and it struck me who she was in his life, I felt something inside me drop, felt my throat swell, found myself turning away and retreating to the curb, in part to protect myself from what I didn't want to believe, mostly because I needed to collect myself, to blink away the tears stinging my eyes, to rearrange my features so as to betray nothing but a distant, impassive stare.

That's what comes back most vividly: the broad midtown New York sidewalks that allowed me, from the start, to proclaim my distance from Christiane.

The four of us proceeded to her small, tastefully appointed East Side apartment, I lagging behind. I stood stiffly by the door, refusing to sit down or touch anything, declining her offer of club soda with a tiny shake of my head, eyes cast down on the mosaics that patterned her wall-to-wall Persian carpet, except when I glowered at Luke for engaging in small talk with her.

On the drive home, I positioned myself in the back seat, hissing insults into my sister's right ear—*four eyes; buck teeth; zit face*—any words that would scald her, that would make her suffer as I was suffering. On school day afternoons, I kicked her bedroom door so many times that after a while it was too warped to close. I shouted and whistled the "Meow Mix" song when she tried to practice the flute.

That she wouldn't sink to my level only made me angrier. The worst she'd do was threaten me. "You're gonna get it when Mom gets home," she'd say. I didn't care. I knew it would be dinnertime before we'd hear my mother's car door slam—soon after my father left, she had enrolled in social work school, two hours away—and more often than not she would be too tired to deal with anything but supper.

It must have been my mother who clocked the six-mile route of steep rolling hills that summer when I decided to go out for the cross-county team. I have no specific recollection of that drive with her, only the four days a week I'd lock my bike to the chain link fence by the high school football field and attack the hills one by one.

One afternoon, heading out the door, I felt a fleck of rain on my cheek. The skies had turned dark. Luke, with whom I'd been bickering all day, told me there was supposed to be a big storm. "Don't be an idiot," she said from the couch before turning her attention back to her thick paperback book.

As I was chaining my bike to the fence, there was a sharp clap of thunder and fat drops of rain began to fall. I fingered the key. I had run the day before; surely one day off wouldn't matter. The rain picked up force, pinging off the steel stadium steps. I imagined riding home, opening the front door, seeing Luke on the couch, her eyebrows raised, *I told you so* smirked on her face.

That was the best run of the summer, and not because I went especially fast, though in the rain or the dark, you always feel as if you're going faster than you really are. But this was a heavy downpour and by the time I got to the bottom of the first hill, my shorts and T-shirt were sopped and my shoes were heavy and sodden and water was running into my eyes.

The thunder boomed, the lightning split the skies, and I had never felt so free. I was contesting the elements. I was streamlining myself into a powerful machine, inured to external forces that threatened to knock me down.

Naturally, that was an illusion. If Christiane materialized on the sidewalk the next day as opposed to ten months before, I'm sure my knees still would have buckled, my newfound fitness notwithstanding. If confronted with a tableful of friends who no longer had a place for me, I would have been no more capable of mustering the courage to ask someone to slide over or, alternatively, telling all of them to go screw themselves.

That didn't matter. At a time when nothing made sense, when I couldn't trust that the ground wouldn't once again shift, I had found something that gave me footing. And, on top of that, made me feel good.

Eventually cross-country and then basketball and track would keep me at school until late, redirect my energies, as my mother would say, and have me lunching with my teammates in the cafeteria. But the damage was done. I spent little time with Luke the years we were in high school together, and while she was at college, just down the road at Yale, she never came home. I used to pop in on her at her dorm in the middle of one of my long training runs, but she treated me warily, as if she couldn't trust that I would not, once again, lash out.

I can't say precisely when Luke let down her guard against me, though I took it as a good sign when she asked me early that spring to be maid of honor at her wedding. Probably it was a gradual process, the passage of time and ventilation of distance slowly and imperceptibly healing the emotional scars inflicted by my rages and wearing down the thick callous she had formed to protect herself against me. My illness worked a further cure, transforming me from bully to patient, and her to protective older sister.

"Hold it," I said, stopping at a clearing and again trying to stretch my back. I groaned. "Jesus, give me my goddamn futon."

"Lise," my sister said. "Forget about the futon. The futon has to be thrown out." It was the finality in her voice that prompted me to press her for an explanation.

She looked down at the dim patches of grass, then to the side. Beyond the stand of trees at the edge of the clearing ranged the black expanse of the Sound. She cleared her throat. "You know it was Christiane who found you, right?"

I nodded. I wasn't sure who told me. Besides that, all I knew was that I had been unconscious in my apartment; I had been rushed to a hospital on the West Side; I was moved to another on the East Side.

"When she found you," Luke said, "which was about noon on Monday, you weren't actually on your futon. You were just below it, on the floor, sprawled. But she said the futon smelled foul, like you'd been lying on it for a long time." She started in the direction of the road, then turned back toward me. "You sure you want me to go on?"

"Go on," I heard myself saying. I felt drained from the walking, but the need to expunge the image of Christiane seeing me in soiled sheets was greater than my fatigue. "Just start from the beginning. I talked to you after my run on Saturday morning. And I must have taken a shower." I always took a shower before a nap. Or had I been too tired? There was something unsettling about my lack of recall, as if, from the time I said good-bye to my sister, my mind, scanning across my memory, showed only black.

When Luke and Cary got home late that afternoon, she tried again. The phone rang and rang.

"I probably disabled my answering machine." It made a loud click if a call came in and invariably woke me up.

My sister knew it was unusual for me to take long naps and when I awakened I would have called her as I said I would. But she brushed off her unease with plausible explanations—I might have gone back to the park or rushed out to a movie or to meet a friend. No doubt my final five days of work would be trying. The last place I'd want to spend that weekend would be in my apartment, brooding and alone.

When there was still no answer on Sunday morning, Luke rang my mother. Something seemed off, she said: I couldn't have been sleeping for that long and if I had gone out, I'd surely have returned her call by then.

"And you told mom not to worry and she said she wouldn't but she would just try me herself?"

"Yup." We were nearing my mother's house. In the distance was the faint sound of waves washing onto the shore. "You okay to keep walking?"

"Fine." I felt caught up in the suspense, as though I were outside myself, watching the events unfold.

My mother hesitated to go on her four-mile Sunday-morning run, a staple of her week, for fear that she might miss my call. Luke told her to go, that if I rang, I would leave a message. But she ended up cutting it short so she could stay near the phone.

At about one, Luke reached my landlord's answering service. She was told he was away for the week and wouldn't be calling in for his messages. And no, my super didn't have a copy of my keys. After the NYPD refused her request to break into my apartment—I hadn't been missing for seventy-two hours and I was neither under eighteen nor over seventy—she was out of ideas. "So I called Dad," she said as we passed a boat hitched to a pick-up truck on the street.

My father was with Christiane and little Marjy at their country house in Connecticut where the three spent each weekend. His efforts to convince the police to intervene did not succeed.

When Luke reported to my mother that we would get no assistance from the NYPD, at about two on Sunday afternoon, my mother telephoned my father.

"Holy shit," I said. Besides a handful of words at graduations and at Luke's wedding, they had not spoken in over two decades.

"Yeah." My sister blew some air through her lips and rolled her eyes at me.

While the two brainstormed on my whereabouts, Luke called a mutual friend of ours, a burly good-natured copy editor at *Newsweek*, who lived on West Twentieth Street. At her request, he took the 9 train up to my apartment, where he hit the buzzer from the street again and again and pounded on the door. When my downstairs neighbor emerged, disturbed, he persuaded her to give him access to the courtyard below my second-floor living-room window. There was no response to his shouts.

Late Sunday afternoon, Luke and my father split up all Manhattan hospitals and called their emergency rooms. I had not been admitted to any of them. By this time my mother was non-functional: she lay on the living-room sofa, her cordless phone beside her, the Sunday *Times* still in its blue plastic sleeve on the coffee table.

That night, my sister and Cary mapped out a plan. Luke had a set of keys to my apartment that she used whenever she took the train from Baltimore to visit. The two would drop off the keys at the railroad station for shipment on the earliest Northeast Amtrak before heading to the hospital Monday morning. Christiane, by then back in New York for work at the United Nations, would pick up the parcel at Penn Station. She would then proceed directly to a police precinct to recruit an officer to accompany her to my apartment. There was no telling what she might find.

"What I don't get," I said, a bit lightheaded, "is why no one considered driving to New York Sunday night."

"Sure I thought about it." My sister looked up at the night sky, her pale features strained, and shook her head, as if still grappling with the question. Crickets chirred. "Honestly?" she said. "Part of me was terrified of what I might find." She kept telling herself there was no guarantee I'd be in the apartment—or that anything was even wrong. It had been only a day and a half since the two of us had talked, after all.

A foghorn sounded in the distance.

"Who knew?" Luke went on. "Maybe you were patching things up with Jake." And then when he didn't answer, that was precisely what she convinced herself: I'd taken off with Jake somewhere, maybe upstate New York, because she remembered we'd gone up there another time, and I'd just show up for work. And then I'd be more annoyed than anything that no one trusted that I could take care of myself.

At half past eight on Monday morning, a bright, pleasant morning, Jake later told me, Luke called my law firm; the receptionist said she had yet to see me come in. An hour later, my father reached my secretary who reported that my office was still dark. Meanwhile, Luke went to work at her Baltimore clinic, her stomach in knots. She canceled her appointments after an hour and returned to their condo where she sat numbly on the couch, waiting for a call.

At about eleven, my stepmother collected the set of keys at Penn Station and rushed to the nearest police precinct. When it became clear that the wait could last for hours, she hailed a taxi and went to my apartment alone. It was there she found me on the floor beside my Stairmaster. I was semi-conscious; my eyes were crossed, my hair was matted; I did not respond when she said my name. She phoned my father to let him know I was in the apartment. She then dialed 911.

When Luke heard from my father that I'd been found, she immediately called my mother. Luke's first words were "She's alive." Once she heard those words, my mother says, she didn't care what came next.

After I hugged Luke and Cary good-bye and watched my mother's Honda disappear down the road the next morning, I went inside and into the study and slid open the top drawer of my mother's desk. I could never know the anguish my family suffered that early-August weekend, I realized, as I unfolded the picture of the cauliflower brain my sister had drawn for me.

Luke would later tell me of my extreme dehydration when I arrived at the hospital Monday afternoon: given the escalating toxicity in my blood after lying unconscious for nearly two days, I probably would not have made it past Tuesday morning. Had she not had a set of my keys and the police waited the full seventy-two hours before breaking into my apartment, had she and my mother not been so sensitized to my uncharacteristic failure to return their calls, had Christiane declined to involve herself, I would be dead.

But even without knowing all that, as I stood staring at the vestigial redness in the right frontal lobe where Luke had symbolically erased away the tumor cells, I felt something like a piercing in my chest that made me breathe sharply inward, some wonder at the power of catastrophe to transmute properties like my sister's maddening reticence into a source of steadiness and strength, and to mobilize a family, no matter how divided the forces.

V

I was on a tear up the hill. Past the two women who were no longer chatting, past Speedo man, past CAN'T STOP GRANNY. Halfway to the top, as the thiry-nine-year-old woman rounded into view, my legs became heavy and stiff and I found myself shifting down. Behind me grew the sounds of grunting, labored breathing, the squeak of gears, the spin of wheels.

I lost focus, felt the air go out of me, the same sensation that overtook me after being summarily rejected for a job teaching elementary Latin at a small private school six months or so after my treatments ended.

By then I had moved on from my nursing aspirations. The teaching gig seemed more in keeping with my background: I wasn't that far removed from my Classics degree and had been studiously reviewing my Latin grammar. *Non legi iam servio.* I am no longer a slave to the law, I rehearsed for my interview. I had a deadpan version and a slyly grinning one. It would depend on the audience. Except I never got one. They wanted someone with teaching experience.

Then came that sense of deflation. Then I had to battle the reflex to assess how far I had fallen off, if I had it in me to keep trying.

And it was no different in this race. Which was why it was so crucial to keep going, keep looking forward. At least until the end. Until I was nearing the finish line and it no longer mattered.

I glanced back. Soon all the ground I had gained would be lost. I waited for my competitive instinct to kick in, for a second wind, a hidden reserve of energy.

Nothing. And I hadn't even passed the nine-mile marker. Still five miles until the run. And then four miles of forcing my tired, wobbly legs onward.

No looking back when you're ill. Little resistance there. It hurts to look back, to see what you've lost, what you may well never recover. No, it's all about looking forward. To the next appointment, the next treatment, to whatever offers that next glint of hope. You look forward with a desperate intensity you've never known. And at times, that's at your peril.

My first appointment with Susan North, my primary oncologist, the Friday before Labor Day, for example. Mid-forties, straight shoulder-length hair the color of stainless steel, beige below-the-knee skirt, brown flats. Short; spare; slight. No frills.

She sat perched on a stool near the door of her examining room, appraising me, my mother, then my father.

"Why don't you tell me what happened?" she said, speech clipped, gaze cool and astringent behind wire-rimmed glasses.

"Hearsay version?" I heard myself asking. "Or just the facts based on personal knowledge?" I felt stronger than I had for weeks—bold, even brash. As though, in the controlled coolness of the examining room, where the messy unknown would finally become as clearly labeled as the laminate drawers, the steps to my recovery as well-calibrated as the instruments on the counter, I could at last reclaim the self I had lost in the last month.

Dr. North looked nonplussed. "I suppose you—"

"Just kidding," I said. "Actually, it all began on a Saturday morning, the first of August . . ."

And so followed my exhaustive account, the frantic phone calls, Christiane finding me, the surgery, the diagnosis. Early on, I couldn't come up with the word "landlord" and paused mid-sentence, tapping my right temple with two fingers.

My mother leaned forward, tried to help.

"No, Martha. Let her tell her story," my father interjected, nostrils flaring. My mother raised her eyebrows, smoothed her hair.

I barely noticed. I was on center stage. I was the witty raconteur, inserting fictional details to round out a scene, shifting to the present tense to make my story more direct and compelling. "So Christiane, my stepmother, she's picked up the keys from Penn Station." Usually I referred to Christiane as my father's wife because there was nothing maternal or motherly about her to me but I was willing to make an exception for dramatic purposes. Plus my father was there, and I was wary of offending him.

"So she's waiting at the police precinct, and they keep telling her an officer will be there soon"—I made an air-quote with my fingers—"and the place—the precinct—is just way too calm," I said, embellishing Luke's version of Christiane's account, and adding some touches from what I'd seen of New York police stations on TV. "There are these beefy cops standing around flirting with a secretary, someone strolls in for directions to Madison Square Garden, and all the while she's just sitting there, waiting in this place, this place that reeks of stale coffee and, worse, stasis."

I did that too, shamelessly dropping in twenty-five cent words here and there. "So she, Christiane, my stepmother, she's thinking to herself, I'm not getting anywhere here and she takes off, hails a cab, and tells the driver, 'no time to lose, West Eighty-second Street, pedal to the metal.'"

I'd never heard Christiane utter any such idiom. She didn't do idioms, as far as I knew. But my father didn't say anything so I went on about her hands shaking as she jerked the key back and forth before the deadbolt clacked and how she pushed open the front door and clopped across the living room in her Bally pumps. "And there I am," I said, letting out a theatrical sigh, "lying on the floor, eyes crossed, hair disheveled, no response when she says my name."

Was it then that it first crossed my mind that Christiane was the one who saved me? That she, the very antithesis of mother, had given me life? To be sure, she wasn't the only one. There was Luke sensing something was amiss and Dr. Schachter, of course, but Christiane was the *sine qua non* of my survival. She barged into my apartment without waiting for the police, she called 911, she sat with me in the harried confines of the ambulance. She didn't have to. She could have asked my father to do it, or at least to go with her. *Sine qua non.* Without her, nothing.

I had no such thought. I was too preoccupied with impressing Dr. North. Which was why I didn't mention that I'd lost control of my bowels as a result of the massive seizure over the weekend and my bedroom no doubt smelled a lot worse than the police station did.

I'm sure she gathered as much. But that didn't matter. The objective was to show her that I was a fascinating study, that she had in me a rare opportunity, given my diagnosis, on which her career might springboard into the stratosphere.

Not that I cared one whit about her career. It was all about me. Still, in order to demonstrate what I could do for her, I couldn't get sidetracked by the profound irony of Christiane's action. This was not the time for a meditation on irony.

And I couldn't act sick or damaged. That's one thing I realized that day: a sick, puling person doesn't generally inspire a doctor's interest or enthusiasm. Nor for that matter does one who's anxious or panicked or, worst of all, resigned to her fate. Doctors are drawn to patients whom they think they can cure. If they succeed, if they compose even one small part of the whole enterprise, it's that much better. It's irrefutable evidence of their worth.

It didn't occur to me that I might be presenting myself to Dr. North as desperate in another way—that is to say, hellbent on getting her to see me as an exceptional patient—and that in itself might have been more tiresome than anything. Or, as turned out to be the case, that none of my efforts to endear myself to her had much effect at all.

I finished my account. "The End," I said, grinning broadly at the three somber faces. No one's expression changed. My father looked pained; his nose twitched. Was everyone thinking "The End" might apply to me? I had to be more careful in the future.

"If . . . your daughter and I could have a few moments." Had she forgotten my name? There was no inflection in her voice. "Standard workup." My mother got up, purse in hand, and headed out. My father followed.

Dr. North pointed to the examining table. I settled myself on the upholstered pad, tearing the crepe paper. "Oops," I said, barking out a laugh.

No response. That was fine. Perhaps there was some sort of policy against engaging in idle conversation with patients or she was too busy drawing the curtain closed.

I tracked her finger with my eyes. She listened to my heart; her stethoscope was cool on my chest. She tested my reflexes, made me resist the weight of her hands pressing against my arms. Her hands felt like dried leaves. At her direction, I slid off the table and walked across the room to the door along a line on the linoleum.

"How 'm I doing?" I asked, turning around to face her. "I'm in pretty good shape, right? I mean, under the circumstances?"

"Hm," she said, removing her glasses and inspecting their lenses. "I suppose." Her eyes were a cold blue, an indifferent patch of sky. She pulled back the curtain and opened the door.

My mother filed in, then my father. My father's pale features appeared hardened. My mother was holding her jaw at an odd angle. I studied the canisters of cotton swabs and tongue depressors on the shelf behind her head.

Dr. North repositioned herself on the stool. She cleared her throat, said nothing. My father slid a notepad and pen from the inside pocket of his jacket. His pen clicked.

My mother folded her arms.

The clock ticked, each tick intensifying my unease. I could make no sense of Dr. North's reserve. Did she think the doctors in New York reviewed the protocol with me before I left? And why were my mother and father so quiet? Had they decided in the hall they would leave the questioning to me?

"The chemotherapy, what about the chemotherapy?" I

finally said, my words spilling out in one exasperated rush.

"Of course," she said. She pushed up the bridge of her glasses with her index finger. Six rounds, one every five weeks, each infusion lasting three to four hours. To begin the following Tuesday, the day after Labor Day.

"That's it?" I asked. "What about side effects? Vomiting? Nausea? Hair loss maybe?"

"Hair loss is less common with BCNU," said Dr. North.

Someone was shouting down the hall. Or laughing. I couldn't tell.

"BCNU?" I asked, pretending to ignore the noise. "Is that short for something?"

"Carmustine." Her beeper sounded. Mechanically she extracted it from the outer pocket of her long white jacket and pressed the button on its side. She scanned its face, looked intently ahead for a moment, replaced it in her pocket.

"Could you spell that?" I asked.

"What?"

"Carmustine," I said, feeling the toe of my right sandal grinding into the linoleum floor.

She spelled it.

"Interesting, the way it's spelled." I had no idea what I meant.

"Any other questions?"

"You were telling me about side effects? Like nausea? Vomiting?"

"Oh yes," she said. "Those may be expected." She glanced at her wristwatch. "Though, actually, there's a new drug. Zofran. The response rate is significantly higher than it was with its precursors."

"Other side effects?" I felt as if I were examining a hostile witness.

"Suppressed white cells, compromised immune system, reduction of platelets," she said, seemingly oblivious to my uncomprehending stare. "Greater susceptibility to bruising.

Lowered crit—hematocrit level." She nodded to herself, as if satisfied she hadn't omitted anything. "Oh, and you're likely to become progressively weaker. Not just directly after the chemo. In between the treatments. Due to the depression of blood counts."

"And if my blood counts go too low? What then?"

"Well, that's why we regularly monitor them," she said, fiddling with her simple wedding band. "In fact, why don't we get a baseline right now? Just down the hall. Ask for Claire. My nurse. She's very good."

Everyone stood up. I didn't. I wasn't ready to leave. Dr. North had come highly recommended, among the top oncologists around, according to Luke. If she was so first-rate, how was it that she exuded so little interest in my case? Was she tired? Overworked?

As Dr. North's beeper went off again, it hit me. What I said or how I acted didn't matter. She didn't think she could cure me, didn't want to invest her energies in a lost cause, didn't want to forge a connection with someone who would soon enough be dead.

Just then, Dr. Schachter's words came back to me: "not necessarily a death sentence, no, absolutely not, not at all . . ." Was that kind of evasiveness and perfunctory attention all I could expect from any doctor involved in my care?

Heat spread to my face. I gripped the sides of my chair. For a moment. Then something in me shifted, something that cooled my face and evened my breathing—again, that impulse toward self-preservation that kept me from learning my prognosis. That, combined with a healthy dose of denial.

I suppose that was how I managed to persuade myself that I needed a little more time to reach Dr. North, even as everyone lingered by the door. I hadn't done enough to show her that I wasn't just another patient with a brain tumor, that my life was that much more worth saving—recite "The Love Song of J. Alfred Prufrock" from memory or juggle the rolls of gauze on the counter or—

"Ready, kid?" my father asked. He and my mother towered over Dr. North; her hand rested on the metal doorknob.

I'd run out of time. And forgotten most of "Prufrock," except "In the room the women come and go/Talking of Michelangelo," and if I uttered those lines out of nowhere, she was liable to think me mad. I wasn't sure I could still juggle, much less rolls of gauze, which are lighter and trickier to control, and it wasn't clear that even standing on my hands would have eked a smile out of Dr. North.

"Can I opt for a trip to Disney World?" I asked as I rose, my voice, in spite of my efforts to stabilize it, rickety.

Dr. North advised against travel in the foreseeable future.

A vast room spread out before us, the fluorescent lighting so glaring I wanted to close my eyes. The three of us stood awkwardly near the entrance, as if just arrived at a busy restaurant. No one appeared to take note of our presence.

Past us a skeletal old man in a wheelchair, eased along by a heavyset nurse, gazed vacantly forward, his chin jutting out like a craggy promontory. In every part of the room people were hooked up to lines: supine on hospital beds; slumped in easy chairs; circulating aimlessly with tall metal racks in tow. A color television on the back wall noised from above.

A sudden sickening rush swept through my gut and took my breath away. This was the oncology ward. *Onkos.* Mass. Tumor. Every person here had one. Or more. I went rigid.

Before, cancer had been an abstraction. Now I saw the face of my disease. It was in the gray skin, the eyes the color of dull pennies, the metallic smell of human sweat and caustic astringent cutting through the air. It was in the limp cotton dressing gowns, the puffy features, the war-survivor stare that seemed to range past the present into some distant indeterminate place. The listlessness that pervaded the room, drained it of energy—I feared it might be contagious. I wanted to flee, go outside, feel the warmth of pure sunlight on my face.

"My daughter's here to have her blood drawn," my father was saying, his voice freighted with professorial gravitas. "By order of Dr. Susan North. Lise?"

My father, his tie loosened, was beckoning to me from the nurses station, sweeping motions that announced he had taken charge of the situation.

"Sweetie," my mother said. Between her and my father stood a slender, red-haired nurse. She was holding a chart against her chest and glancing at the clock.

A phone was ringing. "He's out, drug reaction," someone said in a hurried voice. "We're going to have to admit him. Could you send someone up *stat*?"

I didn't move. I couldn't. The moment I took a step inside, I'd become one of them and, soon enough, indistinguishable from the rest.

"Kiddo." My father.

Then I saw my mother. She was kneading her forehead with two fingers. Her chignon had come undone. A few straggles hung down her neck.

"This is Claire," my father said when I joined them. "Dr. North's nurse." Her face stippled with tiny freckles, she smiled ruefully at me, opening wide her ether-blue eyes and arching her brows. So young, I could hear her saying to herself. What a tragedy. I shook her hand more firmly than necessary.

My mother rested her hand on my sleeveless shoulder. I wriggled away. Shame was creeping over me. This was all wrong. I was too old for her to be mothering me, for me to be dragging her and my father through this mess. In that moment I would have given anything to shake them off, send them anywhere, to the hall, the waiting room, the cafeteria, and endure this bloodletting on my own. I didn't care if they went their separate ways, or suffered each other's company in silence. I just wanted them gone.

Claire led me to a recliner and pulled over a tray table. My mother took a seat on one side, my father the other. I was wearing khaki shorts; the backs of my legs stuck to the dull vinyl.

A La-Z-Boy. What a crock. A hard-backed chair would have been more appropriate. This was business, not relaxation. And the framed prints of Monet's meadows and ponds on the off-white walls—their pastel colors and gentle brushstrokes offered me no solace. Give me Goya's human grotesques grimacing in lunatic frenzy. Give me Caravaggio's snaky-haired Medusa crying out as blood spurts from her neck. Give me anything that told me my fate could be worse, that stopped the self-pity from raining on me, cold and hard.

"But is abstinence a realistic possibility for teens?" a voice brayed from the color television. "I mean, really, people . . ."

All at once I felt a destabilizing whoosh, not unlike the one that used to judder through me as a kid, late at night, when I'd realize that I would not be on this earth forever, that the body I carried around would someday be disintegrating in the ground. But not that often. I guess that's part of growing up, pushing those thoughts off to the side and, as time goes on, assembling a wall between everyday life and the inevitable end. And that wall had largely held up through Dr. Schachter's slippery prognosis and the show of sterile disinterest on the part of Dr. North.

It was in the oncology ward that the first cracks began to break through.

At Claire's direction, I extended my right arm onto the table. Her fingers nimbly climbed up and down every inch in search of one good vein. I watched her mouth hard-set in concentration, the lines finely etched around either side. She shook her head, tried the other arm. "Such lovely fair skin," my mother murmured.

Claire found a vein in the crook of my left arm and burrowed the needle around under the skin. "Am I hurting you?" she asked.

"Dig away," I said. "I'll tell you when you do." I would not tell her. I would not so much as wince. I looked off into space, thrilling to the pain. The ultimate morphine. I wanted her to keep gouging my veins. I did not want the piercing sensation to stop.

It stopped. Claire slid out the needle, clucked her tongue in a rapid staccato. Three or four grudging drops dotted the thin plastic line. Eyes fixed on the paltry result, I felt my fabricated composure crumbling. I envisioned the tumor ravaging that part of my brain that told my blood to flow, wondered which bodily function would be the next to shut down.

"You alright, kid?" My father must have sensed I was about to lose it. I concentrated on the tiny silver cross suspended from Claire's necklace, my throat constricted, willing my eyes to stanch the pooling tears. I gave a small nod.

"What about a port for her, eh?" A guttural rasp. I looked up. Nicotine-stained eyes glazed over me from a recliner across from us. "She needs a port." Scraggly colorless hair, yellowish skin; her wasted body sagged in her seat like a tired paper bag.

"It's a possibility, I suppose," Claire was saying as she tossed the needle into a receptacle labeled MEDICAL WASTE behind her.

"A port?" My mother.

"That's right," said Claire. "It's a sort of hollow flexible tube and we'd implant it in her upper chest. That's where you find the larger veins. It might be an idea. We could use it for drawing blood and also for the chemotherapy infusions. And we could probably fit her in this—"

"Hello?" I said, roused by my irritation at Claire's reference to me in the third person. "Do I have any say in this?"

"Of course you do," said Claire. "Hold one moment." Someone was summoning her to the nurses' station. "It'll be a few minutes," she called out. "This one's got no veins." She turned up her palms and shook her head. "SHE'S GOT NO VEINS."

"And you can take a shower with it, and it doesn't even hafta be covered," the crone was saying.

I turned to my father. "What is this lady, on the port company payroll or something?" I said under my breath. "Because there's no way I'm—"

My father patted my knee. "Surely there are alternatives," he said to Claire.

"No, no," said the woman, shaking her head. "No, trust me. This is what she should have. Here, lemme show you." With trembling fingers, she unfastened the top two buttons of her graying pink blouse, exposing a short piece of tubing sticking out of the right side of her mottled chest. Her cleavage was an ancient dried-up gully.

"Thanks, but I'm not sure—"

"Nothing to be afraid of, young lady," she was saying through strings of phlegm. "Had it put in last November. Operation's a cinch; they just put you in a sort of twilight. Y'know, like *The Twilight Zone*."

She cackled; I didn't know why. Or she might have been hacking because she continued even after I told Claire that I needed time to mull it over. "Let's try once more," I said, voice tiny, the world shrunk to the needle and the crook of my arm.

Claire returned with a smaller needle. "We usually save these for the kids," she said, then asked if I minded her looking for a vein on the back of my hand. "Some people are fussy about their hands," she explained.

"Try anything," I said.

VI

Just over the brow of a hill, a stationary figure was stooped over. The guy in the Speedo. His hands were on his thighs and he was struggling to catch his breath. "Hand pump?" he panted in a heavy German accent, gesturing at his flattened front tire as gloom spread across his sculpted features.

I shook my head, trying to avert my eyes from the Speedo, and continued along.

And then, after a house or two, I stopped pedaling, just let the bike glide down a mild decline, feeling on the outside of my shorts for the cylindrical CO_2 cartridge for reinflating a flat tire in my pocket. Sure, the cartridge could only be used once and the odds were slim I'd get a flat in the last four or five miles. Besides, considering my only objective was to finish and my time was of no relevance, there was every reason to loop back around and toss it in his direction.

I kept coasting. It was too late and I was too spent to turn back, I told myself, fighting against my better instincts, fighting back that gnawing awareness that I was no better, no nobler for what I had endured.

And it wasn't only this. I could have used the unlikelihood of my recovery to inspire others or to advocate for cancer research or for some other unsung cause. I hadn't. I wanted no part of that world. I hadn't even taken the first steps toward pursuing nursing.

Yes, I was a so-called survivor, but who among the living wasn't? The scar ranging across the side of my scalp, the slightly receded hairline, and the knowledge that I had undergone a difficult trial: that was all I had to show for what I'd been through. That, some writing fellowships, and a fledgling job as a freelance reporter for the local paper.

I cruised past a sign on a front lawn. PRICE RE-DUCED! BANK OWNED! it read. I was making too much of this, spending too much time second-guessing myself. This wasn't a real problem. In any event, either it would dissolve from my memory or get snagged on something and resurface later. Either way, the distance between Speedo guy and me was already too far.

I set my feet back on the pedals and started off.

My great aunt Adele would have approved. Outside the Reisman family, my father's paternal aunt had little patience for altruism. *What are you now, a saint?* she would have asked in her thick nasal whine, clad in a stylish raincoat, a transparent plastic wrap covering her impeccably upswept hair. *What do you owe this man? And a German, no less? You just take care of yourself and keep going.*

Adele had died at seventy-nine in 2000, eight years before, but the strident tone of conviction in whatever she proclaimed still resounded.

"You're not feeling so good, are you?" I remember her saying the Monday night that Labor Day weekend was coming to a close, her shrill rising as if to cover the distance between Yonkers and my mother's house in Connecticut. She had learned about my condition from my father in the middle of August and had been phoning me from time to time ever since. "I can hear it in your voice," she continued. "Your voice sounds like there's nothing in you."

"I'm dealing." I eyed *Love, Medicine & Miracles,* a self-help book the paralegal Dotie had sent me. Apart from a call from my secretary about a missing file, I hadn't heard from anyone else at the firm. For a while I found myself waiting for the phone to ring; for a time I'd feel a flash of anger at the seeming disinterest once the height of mortal drama had subsided. But then I wondered if I could blame them; I wasn't even sure I'd reach out to someone I knew who might be dying. Or for that matter what I would say if someone did phone. Would anyone really want to hear me detail the pros and cons of a port? Which was why I screened Jake's calls and only returned his messages on his home phone in the middle of a work day to tell him I was doing fine.

"You're not eating enough," Adele was saying. "I can tell." From the back cover a bald man with a resemblance to a cult leader smiled up at me, his eyes benign with compassion. There was something unctuous about his smile. So much so that I couldn't take in a passage I read and reread, about the power of hope, about the importance of flooding myself with positive thoughts.

"You're just like your father and your father's just like your grandfather," she went on. Adele was my grandfather's youngest sister. "You forget to eat and then you start thinking bad thoughts. You need to eat more. Protein. You eat more protein, you'll feel better, have better thoughts."

My mother tiptoed into the study and flicked on the desk lamp.

"Okay," I said. Adele was right. By then I was off the Decadron. I had no appetite. My growing dread of meeting my radiation oncologist the next morning wasn't helping. I kept imagining him as a male incarnation of Dr. Susan North.

"Let me give you one more bit of advice, honey," Adele was saying.

My mother slid a dog-eared copy of *Full Catastrophe Living* from the middle of a stack of books, the same book I'd dismissed with a haughty wave of my hand when she offered it earlier that week. That gave me a charge, my show of contempt, perversely made me feel a bit less pathetic.

The hardwoods creaked under her sandals as she closed the door behind her.

"You listening to me, dear?"

"I'm listening."

"I want you to start sprucing yourself up," Adele said. "You have a big day tomorrow, an appointment, then your first treatments, radiation, chemo, am I right? So what should you do? Get a little dressed up, put on some lipstick, a little rouge, you and your sister, you're such beautiful girls, you never wear makeup. You'll feel better. Mark my words. And you have to eat. Just what I said, you're not eating enough. So have your mother make you some nice eggs and bacon for breakfast," she said. "And the lipstick. Don't forget about the lipstick."

Maybe it was the infusion of fried eggs and sausage; maybe it was my relief the next morning that the boyish-looking, upbeat guy charging into the reception area was no Dr. North.

All I know is that the moment I shook Dan Quigley's hand—it was warm and dry, and below his rolled-up sleeves the tendons stood out of his forearm like spokes—I could hear my voice changing key, as if from minor to major.

"How can you prove you're my doctor," I asked as my mother and I followed him down the hall, "when all you have to show for yourself is that stethoscope?" Upon which, with a sly grin, he scoffed at the pretentiousness of white jackets.

At the front desk, his secretary beamed at him, then at me and my mother. "Hi, Lisa!" she said. "I'm Misty." She had taffy-colored hair and large front teeth that cheerfully protruded over her lower lip. Dr. Quigley was a few steps ahead, rhapsodizing to my mother about radiation oncology, saying it was his passion.

"If it's your passion," I called up to Dr. Quigley as I waved see-you-later to Misty, "what exactly is it that you do for fun?" I caught my reflection in the glass case of a fire extinguisher, checked my lipstick.

"Orthography," he replied. He had been National Spelling Bee champion in 1971.

And then we were in his exam room and he was throwing back his head and rocking with laughter when I told him I was a recovering lawyer and he was welcome to sit in on the meetings every Wednesday evening in the local church basement, and as he was going on to my mother about the fresh steamers at Bud's, the celebrated fish market in her town, I was thinking *yeah, baby*.

Whatever he might tell us about my condition and my survival became secondary. This was Dr. Quigley's magic, at least on that day. He laughed at my jokes. He treated me as if I were normal and not compromised. That's the worst part of having some dread disease—feeling vulnerable and scared and, more than anything, a diminished version of who you once were.

The trick was to act as if I were well, to the extent that was possible. And that was only feasible if others were complicit in the production. In this Dr. North fell short. But Dr. Quigley, it seemed, was all in.

Particularly when he leaned toward me on his green stool, gently tapping his left hand against my knee just below the frayed hem of my cutoff jeans—there was no ring—and inquiring about the history of the scars I had amassed from countless scrapes and falls as a kid.

"From the war," I said, his touch sending a flare through me. He smelled like soap.

Ten minutes later, my father joined us, apologizing that he had been detained at the law school and settling himself on a chair by the door, the pants of his slate-gray suit rumpled, before nodding at my mother across the room. I cringed at the oversized briefcase on the luggage cart he wheeled in behind him. Why couldn't he just carry a regular attaché case?

The rest of the appointment comes back to me only dimly, as if my whole system, unable to bear the overload, had switched over to emergency lighting. My mother nervously smoothing her hair as the doctor and my father exchanged pleasantries. Her thumb and forefinger touching the bridge of her nose when Dr. Quigley told us the tumor had been about the size of a golf ball. Her eyes half-closing when he added that it was mostly of a low grade and its location was such that neither my sight nor my motor functions were likely to have been damaged.

That was when Dr. Quigley squinched his face and rubbed his ear. "On the other hand, we also have highly malignant cells in the middle of the mass—grade 4 cells," he said.

"Which means?" I felt heat rising to my face.

"Which means," he said, puffing his cheeks and letting his breath out slowly, "the most malignant, the most aggressive."

Grade 4. Most malignant. Most aggressive. I'd heard those words before, but this time, conveyed as they were in such startling contrast to Dr. Quigley's buoyant demeanor, they hung in the air like some heavy noxious cloud, leaving me with the sensation that I was falling headlong into nothing.

"You have to remember," Dr. Quigley was saying. "Diagnosis doesn't necessarily signify prognosis."

My mother, her legs tucked under her chair, scribbled his last pronouncement on the back of an envelope, and underscored it, emphatically, three or four times.

"But if, as you say, Dr. Schachter resected ninety-nine percent of the tumor," my father was saying, "logically we should infer that he got the grade 4 cells in the middle, should we not?" His voice was hoarse, more so than I remembered, and for the first time I noticed his haggard face, the careworn features. My father, so alive, so intense, you could almost feel his synapses crackling, my remarkably vigorous father, who worked out for an hour in the gym after a fourteen-hour day— writing at dawn; teaching classes; meeting with his law students; editing journals—now splayed in his chair, resting his head against the wall, his eyes now like an old man's, watery, the color drained out of them.

I hadn't seen him since the appointment with Dr. North the week before, only talked to him each night briefly on the phone, hadn't paused to reflect how hard he might be taking this—his daughter with a malignant brain tumor.

Tears stung my eyes; I quickly blinked them away.

"We can't afford to assume anything," Dr. Quigley was saying. "Particularly in a case like this." And pushing away the lank sandy-brown hair that fell across his forehead, he launched into an extended analogy of the problem, my father taking notes, my mother listening intently, me imploring myself to regain my composure.

Masking tape and lint and sweaters. That's what I chiefly remember of what he said. The same way one might use masking tape to pick lint off a sweater but inadvertently leave behind some flecks, Dr. Schachter could have removed most of the mass but missed some grade 4 cells too microscopic to be seen. But there the analogy ended: unlike the flecks on the sweater, the malignant cells, if left alone, would divide and multiply.

"So," I said. The word came out rough, rutted. My throat had gone dry. I swallowed hard. "Given that masking tape is out of the question, what do we do to make sure the flecks don't spread?"

Dr. Quigley's sea-green eyes glimmered. "Six weeks of radiation, three rounds of chemo," he said, glancing at my chest. Another flare. "Radiation, every day, starting today. Just show up. You may feel a little tired afterwards and there might be some hair loss but trust me—it's worth it. In December we'll see if there's been any regrowth. The December MRI is pretty much pivotal. If it's clean, we're okay."

I can't describe with much coherence the feeling that overtook me for the rest of the day. It still doesn't make sense—Dr. Quigley hadn't offered any guarantees; in fact, he as much as confirmed my worst fears, that tumor cells might be spreading through my brain, even then, as I made my way along the corridor and back down the flight of stairs to the radiation clinic for my first treatment, my mother and father trailing behind me.

But there it was, a visceral sense of relief, as if, after weeks of treading water in a foggy mist of half-seen apparitions and faint soundings of doom, I could finally glimpse the demarcations of a rescue vessel.

It's really quite simple, it's occurred to me since then, and it doesn't matter if you're stuck in a burning building or on a plane about to make a crash landing. When confronted with grave danger, people crave authority and direction. Not just any authority and direction. That's where those passages I'd looked at in the self-help book the night before disappointed and Adele's exhortation to eat protein and apply lipstick worked. Thinking positive thoughts and instilling myself with hope wouldn't tell me how to get onto the life boat. Adele and Dr. Quigley did.

I forgot about Dr. North and the twilight lady in the cancer ward. I ignored the dark reaches beyond the December MRI. When a bald sallow-skinned woman—somewhere between thirty and sixty—limped into the radiation clinic waiting room with a cane, her clothes hanging over her emaciated frame like drapes, and nodded at me as she subsided into her chair, I didn't look away for fear that her image would awaken me late at night or during my weakest moments. I composed myself, looked her square in the eye, and smiled. And when my name was called, I strode briskly into the radiation room, my demonstration—why and to whom I didn't know—that I was vigorous and strong.

And then I felt it: after I lay down under the hood of the massive cobalt machine; after the radiation therapists fit a white plastic mask over my head and riveted it to the pallet so that I could only look upward; after I fixed my eyes on the ceiling tiles; after I started at a high-pitched chirring that lasted at most five seconds and drew a deep breath to calm myself, there it was: a sudden onrush of exhilaration that coursed through me and the words I murmured out loud but more to myself: *Let's do this.*

As if the beams of radiation were still sending waves through my system, I surged across the street and into the oncology ward, lipstick intact, eyes straight ahead, barely registering the creatures wandering around the room like commuters waiting endlessly for a train and weary of sitting still.

I poked my head into the nurses' station and asked for Claire. "Name's Reisman," I said as my mother caught up to me. "Dr. North's patient. First day of chemotherapy. One o'clock appointment." My father had stopped at a kiosk to get me a sandwich.

The place was bedlam: no easy chairs without occupant, newspaper, jacket. Claire led my mother and me past an empty stretcher to an alcove off the main ward. "This looks like your only choice," she said. "If something in the main area opens up—"

"It's fine," I said. It could not have been better. Claire dashed off.

My father emerged from the front of the ward, a paper bag in one hand, wheeling his oversized briefcase behind him. My mother, front section of the Tuesday *Times* and *When Bad Things Happen to Good People* under her arm, stood up. "So about an hour?"

My father looked at his watch. "That should be fine," he said coolly.

Claire reappeared, rolling a cart in front of her and nodding at my mother as she exited the alcove.

"All ready?" asked Claire.

"Never more," I said.

"Yeah, baby." My father was grinning. This wasn't an expression he ordinarily used. He must have picked it up from little Marjy. Luke and I had taught it to her during the wedding weekend back in June, I recalled just then.

Claire gently slapped the insides of each of my arms. Before I could suggest one of the methods I had experimented with the night before—a rubber band wound so tightly around my arm that it left a welt; the hottest water I could bear to swell my veins—she found one just below the base of my thumb and rigged me up to the IV tubing. The tubing extended to a bag of clear fluid hanging from a metal rack.

To plump up my veins, I'd been doing sets of crunches with a five-pound free weight, each arm, every evening, ever since the old woman tried to sell me on the idea of a port. It was Luke's suggestion and it might have worked, hot water or not. Anything to avoid a tube dangling from my chest, the material reminder, each time I noticed it in the shower or felt it pressing against my shirt, that I had cancer in my brain. I would never get used to that. I couldn't let myself.

"This is Zofran—the anti-nausea medication?" Claire said.

I nodded. "Always happy for a little anti-nausea," I said as it began its downward drip into the IV tubing.

Her mouth hyphenated into a tight close-lipped smile. She was focused on the trajectory of the drip. For a moment I felt for her. All day she doubtless had to tolerate patients trying to dispel their anxiety with lame jokes.

"I'll be back," she said. She hurried into the main ward.

Twenty minutes later, Claire replaced the empty bag with a pouch of clear solution and a bottle of fluid. I liked the way she didn't ask how I was feeling, just assumed I was doing fine. And how she went about her job, efficient, no-nonsense; I liked that too. It seemed so natural and satisfying, tending to patients, reassuring them just by doing what she did well.

"So this is the saline," she said as she turned the bottle upside down and attached it to the top of the metal rack.

"What does it do?" I observed her intently as she flipped open the valve, imagining myself, perhaps by my third or fourth round of chemo, trailing her discreetly around the ward, a sort of patient-intern. Maybe this turn of misfortune was part of a larger plan. Maybe I was meant to be a nurse all along.

"The BCNU tends to burn as it goes through the veins," Claire was saying. "The saline dilutes it."

The poison inched through the plastic line into my bloodstream. I watched the bottle slowly draining, the fluid creeping down the line. What a passive procedure. My knees bounced up and down, same as when I'd sprained my pinky near the end of the basketball season in my sophomore year of high school. Hours upon hours of practice, flush with excitement before each game, and each game languishing on the bench, cheering on my teammates, yearning to be part of the action.

I wanted to do something, anything, and now I couldn't even rally the forces from the sidelines. I closed my eyes and tried to picture the fluid sluicing through the pathways of my veins, asphyxiating the malformed, deviant cells, leaving them choking, writhing, guttering, dead.

"You okay, kid?" My father's head was bent over a thick stack of pages.

"Fine." I didn't mind that he was working. He was always working on something—a manuscript, an article, a legal opinion, a lecture. I was just happy to be sitting next to him. When was the last time the two of us were by ourselves? "Hey Dad, you know what I just remembered?" I heard myself saying. "Going to sleep to the tapping of your typewriter. To this day, that sound, it's as soothing as a lullaby."

He chuckled, then crossed out a phrase with a single line.

"What sentence did you just doom to extinction, anyway?"

His face turned to a grimace. "Copy-editing." He was serving his term as editor of the *American Journal of International Law*, he said, and some of the administrative duties had devolved to him.

"Send some pages over here," I said. My mind felt preternaturally clear. No grogginess, nausea, confused thinking. Nothing.

He handed me a few. Something about a boundary dispute between Cameroon and Nigeria.

"This is the bestseller I've been hearing about?" I asked. "The one keeping everyone up until three in the morning?"

My father smiled and bent his head back to his work.

A nurse pushed a cart of box lunches toward me. She moved slowly, like thick syrup across a pancake.

"No thanks," I said, pointing at the wrapped sandwich from the kiosk.

"I'll have hers," sang out a plump short-haired woman across from us. Besides a small nod when I'd entered the alcove, I had not given her notice. With her chubby forearm, she nudged aside her *Reader's Digest* and a Snickers wrapper crumpled up on the tray table in front of her.

"If you want anything to drink . . ." The nurse gestured across the room to a cube-shaped refrigerator. The woman pushed away her tray and heaved herself to her feet with a soft grunt. Presently she returned to the alcove with a Coke and a cup filled with ice.

"Just let me know if you need anything, honey," the nurse said to me. Her identification tag read MARY BROWN.

"Hey Dad? Not to keep tripping down memory lane but you remember Mary McCool?" It was a reference to a song we used to chant as we strolled each evening under the oaks that arched over our street after he got home from work. I hadn't thought about that for a long time.

"Of course I do, kiddo." My father looked off into the middle distance and grinned. "I'd drive up our hill and there you'd be on the front stoop waiting for me. Highlight of my day."

"Ma-ry Mc-COOL," I began in a sort of jive talk. "Mary Mc-COOL."

"Mary-Mary-Mary-Mary-Mary Mc-COOL," he rejoined.

"Yup," I said. "Good ol' Mary," and then felt, as I did when reflecting on the years our family was whole, an ache of sadness for what had been lost.

I went back to the article. I had read the first two sentences three times.

An hour later, my mother entered the ward. I observed her long stride, her slim-fitting hunter-green suit, and noted, with some pride, how striking her features remained at fifty-nine. Odd, how much I wanted my father to see my mother flourishing, see that she had lived and thrived without and despite him, whatever the disdain I'd been feeling toward her when we were alone.

My father got up. I bowed my head so he could kiss its crown. He kissed Luke and Pip the same way. No hugs ever, as far as I could recall, since we were little kids. Back then he'd hug us the way he hugged Marjy now. Maybe there was some kind of cutoff age.

"Good-bye, Martha," he was saying, no trace of warmth in his voice.

"Wait," I heard myself saying, and just then, as I slid back the metal pole and rose carefully so as not to disengage the IV, I felt like throwing up. It wasn't from the chemo; it was more a kind of motion sickness, as though, standing between my mother and father, I was pitching and rolling on my shifting loyalties. "I'll walk you out," I said to my father.

We reached the hall. "So I'll talk to you tonight?" he asked.

I looked down at the linoleum, still unsteady. I didn't want my father just to leave. I wanted to say it meant a lot that he'd stayed with me and I might need him to reprise that role for the next round. And also to tell him I was sorry for getting sick and I'd be okay and not to worry.

I couldn't. I didn't want to cry. I had to show him I was strong. "Sorry for not eating the sandwich," I said in a little voice, still looking down.

"That's alright, kid." My father patted my shoulder.

"You won't believe this," my mother said when I came back from the corridor a few minutes later, guiding the metal pole past the array of flyers posted on the stucco walls.

LYMPHOMA GROUP UPDATE!

LOST CHORD CLUB:
A SUPPORT GROUP FOR PEOPLE WHO HAVE HAD
LARYNGECTOMIES.

"Sandra's son works in Manhattan. On Wall Street." My mother had been chatting with the woman who ate my boxed lunch. I tried to affect interest, asked where he lived, what firm he worked for. The son and I had nothing in common.

I paged through a pamphlet on wigs and hats for women who had lost their hair. Sandra had breast cancer and recently suffered her second recurrence, I overheard. Since starting on a new chemotherapy regimen, she couldn't stop eating. "Twenty-seven pounds," she said, heaving a sigh and shaking her head. "I can barely tie my shoes anymore."

Sandra did most of the talking, my mother leaning toward her, as she would one of her students, clarifying, empathizing, drawing out her story. From time to time, I caught Sandra eyeing me.

I had retreated into silence. I would not communicate with her. Any further contact would have led to what she no doubt saw as our primary shared trait: the disease. I knew otherwise. If we'd happened to stop at the same rest station, this Sandra and I, we were traveling in opposite directions. She could not help me on my way and neither could I on hers.

Three hours after the treatment began, the drips ceased; the bag was empty. Claire set me free. "See you in October," I said, tossing the wig pamphlet in the trash and high-fiving my mother as we tripped out of the oncology ward.

Back at the house later that afternoon, I went out for a short run, a defiant run, the first time I'd run since July, since before the surgery, since before the tumor announced itself that early August weekend. Defiant because I would not let the treatments sap my energy and gnaw away my will. Defiant because, far from being plagued by fatigue following radiation or racked with nausea in the wake of the chemotherapy, I felt better than I had for weeks. Defiant because for that one day at least, I had the momentum.

VII

The numbness spread from my cheeks, to my lips, my tongue, then into my hands and fingers. My vision went double. Cold sweat streamed down my face. I had overtaxed myself on the hills.

I kept pedaling. This kind of spell always passed, I knew. I just had to ride it out. Though I'd never had one on my bike. Or during a workout.

The first of three had come six weeks earlier, around the time of my tenth anniversary. I was leaning against my couch on the floor of my cottage, legs outstretched, chewing on a sesame bagel. I had cycled thirteen miles, then run four. In the bright August light, something small was lying outside on my deck. I blinked my eyes and focused. It was a bird.

All of a sudden, a shock went through my head and into my fingertips and toes. A seizure? I'd had only one, ten years before, and I had no memory of it.

A dead bird and a seizure to mark my tenth anniversary.

Beautiful. Heart gonging, I braced myself against the couch, and squeezed my eyes shut, my lips now slack, my tongue deadened, my fingers tingly and useless.

I felt the warmth of sun on my face. Then it went dark. I started, clenched my teeth. Just as suddenly, the light returned. It must have been a cloud passing. I smelled the sesame seed on the bagel, heard a train's whistle in the distance.

At some point my heartbeat slowed. I opened my eyes. The numbness was receding. It hadn't been a seizure. The bird was gone. It must have flown into my window and fortuitously landed on my deck, where it could regain its bearings.

I told no one about it, just as I kept to myself the dizzy spells and the shafts of pain through my head and the blurry vision. They came and went, after all.

Surviving a serious illness was a gift, to be sure. It was also a burden. *Deinos* all over again. Awful and awesome; terrible and wonderful. If I complained about every ache and twinge, it would only compound the distress I'd caused everyone close to me. It also might take the shine off the unlikelihood of my survival.

"GO JASON!" shouted a group of girls from the side of the road to a guy just in front of me.

I kept pedaling—it was the stretch before the fork in the road that led to the transition area—and considered an alternative: I was bonking. The word in cycling synonymous with hitting the wall. It happens when the muscles run out of fuel. It's the body saying, in short, I have no more to give. I'm about to shut down.

I kept pedaling.

"Suggest an alternative," I remember my sister saying on the Sunday night before my third week of treatments. Cary's mother had volunteered to drive me to the radiation center. "Mom's out of the question. She won't admit it, but she's worn out from all the back and forth to New Haven."

"Has she said anything?" A few mornings before, I had taken her to task for failing to water one of her house plants. "I need to look at a dying plant all day?" I said, my words barbed, as she fixed me a sandwich for lunch. On the drive to the radiation clinic the next afternoon, I'd grumbled about the rank smell in her car. It was from an old banana peel. "Revolting," I said, regarding the crumbs on the carpet under my sandals, the smudged makeup under her eyes, her creased silk pants. Careless; imperfect; letting things slide. If this was my legacy—and how it could not be, at least in part, given the mess that was now my life—I had to fight against it, and the easiest way was to scorn her, to make her the problem.

"You just can't take her for granted, Lise," Luke was saying.

I shifted the receiver to my left hand and set down the collection of poems I'd been studying in the quiet light of the study. My mother had gone food shopping. "What—Christiane wasn't available?" I hadn't seen my stepmother since Luke told me how she had saved my life. Not that I minded. I wasn't sure what I would say or what effect, if any, her rescue might have on our strained relations. Plus it didn't seem particularly urgent.

"Very funny," Luke said. "You really need to give Mom a break."

"I hear you," I said, "but does Cary's mother even drive?" I summoned a picture of Helene carrying her diminutive frame with mincing steps in dainty pumps. She tended toward the frilly dress from what I'd seen at the various family gatherings surrounding the June wedding. She had worked at IBM at some point; I wasn't sure in what capacity. And though she must have been nearing sixty, her perfect ivory complexion made her appear oddly well-preserved, as if she hadn't really lived.

That was my image of Helene that Sunday night. I also recalled a photo from a series of wedding snapshots Luke had shown me during the August week she and Cary stayed in Connecticut. In the center is my mother, captured mid-shimmy in a circle of hora dancers, her champagne-colored dress accentuating her dark eyes, her gold evening bag suspended in the air; there is an expression of dazzling joy on her face. In the far right corner, slightly out of focus, Helene, mother of the groom, leans against the wall, her light-blue ruffled gown cut off by someone's outstretched tuxedoed arm.

Pale, meek, passive—definitely not what I needed. What I needed was someone from whom I could draw strength, who would keep me on pace, who would block out any distractions that might hinder my recovery. "It's really nice of her," I heard myself saying, "but—"

"Helene's great," Luke said in a voice that would accept no contradiction. "You just have to get to know her."

When I tentatively opened the passenger door of the boat-like Lincoln Continental on the bright afternoon Helene picked me up for my Monday treatment, the poodled hair and flouncy blouse all comported with the picture I had been dreading since the night before. Of course, I had never been driving with Helene, so the fuzz buster on her dashboard did give me pause. As did the bumper stickers displayed prominently on the back fender—I SUPPORT THE POUGHKEEPSIE POLICE FORCE and THIS MOTHER BACKS THE LOCAL SHERIFF'S ASSOCIATION.

"Don't knock it," she said in her girlish voice when I questioned her on the selection of stickers. "Those and a few words of appreciation for the officers' hard work and dedication have saved me hundreds." And sitting pert and petite in her soft-leather driver's seat, she batted her eyelashes and giggled.

Because of the fuzz buster, it seemed, Helene had no need to allocate the usual hour to drive from her brother's house in Stamford, where she was staying for the week. I learned this on Tuesday, when her car heaved into the driveway at 3:37, twenty-two minutes after we had arranged for her to arrive. My appointment was at 3:45. The clinic was fifteen minutes away.

I wiped some sweat from my forehead as Helene was going on about a bottleneck, and tried to quiet the pounding in my head. I had been pacing up and down the stretch of lawn near the road, counting the cars that sped by. *Ten cars*, she'll be here, I told myself, hands balled into fists in the pockets of my jeans. Ten cars passed, then another ten; at some point, I stopped counting and stood stock-still by the mailbox, convinced that Helene wouldn't show up at all, that missing one treatment would compromise the entire radiation process, cursing my mother for being too exhausted to drive me, and my sister for forcing Helene onto me, glaring at the SUVs barreling by for polluting the air with their fossil fuels. "You just have to understand—these treatments are it for me these days. They're basically what's keeping me going."

Helene raised the tips of her fingers to her lips. "And here I came to help." She shut her eyes tight and shook her head, as if rebuking herself, then consulted her watch. "Seven minutes." She centered herself behind her steering wheel with a little grunt; her chin was about level with the bottom of the wheel. And flying down the highway at roughly eighty-five mph, she delivered us to the radiation clinic at 3:44.

"Whew," she said, collapsing into the seat beside me and parking her pocketbook and canvas bag on the carpet. "I was okay until that final sprint from the lot. These legs haven't felt that kind of burn since my Jane Fonda aerobics videotape from the eighties." She patted a lace handkerchief around her brow and flapped her sleeves up and down.

"Well done," I said between my teeth, wondering how I would endure her for the rest of the week and, if I couldn't, whether I could persuade Luke to let me take a taxi to and from the clinic. How hadn't I thought of that before?

I glanced at the pasty-faced man in the chair across from us in the low-ceilinged room and inwardly groaned. As usual, his head was tilted against the wall, his red-rimmed eyes were closed, and his mouth was open; I could hear the air pass through his throat like a dry wind. He was wearing the same rumpled suit and stained white sneakers he'd worn every day in my two weeks of treatments. The dour-looking middle-aged woman shuffled in and sat down heavily, a gold cross suspended from a heavy chain over her plain black tunic.

Helene leaned down and pulled out a wrinkled newspaper from her bag. "I get behind," she explained when she saw me eyeing the date on the local section of the *Poughkeepsie Journal*. The dateline on the paper read May 29. I wasn't sure she was serious.

Ruby, one of the radiation technicians, appeared with her clipboard and rosy smile. "Don't you look pretty today," she said, as she did in some form or other every day. She beamed at Helene. We headed into the treatment room.

"Not mine," I said after Ruby commented that my mother-in-law seemed sweet. "My sister's. She's just trying to help us out." Emphasis on trying, I thought, as I took off my cap and lay down on the table before Ruby fitted the plastic mesh mask over my head.

When I alighted from my treatment, Helene was deep in conversation with the middle-aged woman. I stood by the magazine rack several feet away until Helene noticed me.

"What a nice lady," she said as we crossed the parking lot, the strong autumn sunlight dancing off her Jackie O sunglasses. There were two treatment rooms; the woman had the same 3:45 appointment as mine. Evidently she had stayed to continue her discussion with Helene. "Very spiritual. You really should talk to her."

"No thanks." I opened the door and eased myself into the passenger seat. I felt a bit woozy, as if I'd been out in the sun too long. "This is business," I said, blinking hard to clear my head. "I'm not at the clinic to make friends." I fastened my seatbelt and pushed down the lock.

Tuesday was the day Helene gifted me the crystals. "Just follow the directions on the bag," she chirped when we arrived at the house. "They're supposed to accelerate healing." The next day, she reached behind her seat and produced a Barnes & Noble shopping bag as we lingered in the driveway after my treatment.

"Wow, Helene," I said. "This is really too much." I knew she was trying, but I was already feeling that resigned exasperation that came with finding in the mailbox another self-help book on living with cancer or recipe for fighting cancer or article on someone surviving cancer, a dread that their steady accretion threatened to wall me into the world of my illness. And yet something kept me from throwing anything out, some need to be reminded that, even if a phone call might be too much, people were thinking of me, that I hadn't been entirely forgotten.

A screen door slapped shut from the house next door, followed by a shriek of laughter. The little girls next door.

"Look," I said. "You have to believe this, you're doing enough, driving me back and forth and keeping me company. You must see how few people I deal with these days. Basically, it's you and the radiation people and my mom—"

"I know," Helene said, gazing ahead. "It's just . . ." She had her two sons, and Luke and her other daughter-in-law, but they all lived far away. Since retiring from IBM, she was usually alone. She had her projects around the house, of course, and she was thinking of signing up for ballroom dancing lessons, but helping people gave her a sense of purpose. "Maybe that's why I sometimes go too far," she said, turning to me. Her small cornflower-blue eyes were full. "It's my chance to do something." She looked lovely at that moment.

"I get it," I said.

Moose leapt onto the hood with a soft thud.

"Now," she said, lifting the bag toward me.

It was a plastic-covered audiobook titled *Peace, Love, and Healing*. Beneath it, a paperback: *From Victim to Victor*. I turned it over.

FIGHT CANCER TOGETHER WITH YOUR
PHYSICIAN AND OTHER HEALTH CARE
PROFESSIONALS!
FIGHT CANCER TOGETHER WITH OTHER
CANCER PATIENTS
YOU ARE NOT ALONE!

I cringed and told her they looked great.

"The first one I thought you could listen to on your walks," Helene said, cracking open the car door. On our drive home the day before, I had described my daily routine—walking, practicing piano, and memorizing poetry. In the midst of organizing my mother's bookshelves one rainy day before radiation, I had chanced on *The Top 500 Poems* and resolved to learn at least one poem a week by heart, as much to exercise my mind as to revel in the language. At Helene's request, I recited a few lines from "Stopping by Woods on a Snowy Evening" and she had clapped her hands with glee.

"I think I'll just retire into the arms of Morpheus for now," I said once we got inside. I felt dulled, as if the radiation had overcooked my brain. It also could have been my walk that morning, almost two miles. Or one of my medications.

There was no way to know. In neurology, I would learn, there can be more than one plausible explanation for a sensation but not enough facts to distinguish between them. The trouble was that there would be no facts until the December MRI. Not to mention that any stress would almost inevitably be felt most keenly in the weakest area—in my case, where the tumor had been removed.

Helene propped her bag against the armrest of the patchwork chair. "Then I'll just let you and Morpheus have at it," she said.

"Thanks for that, but can I trust you down here?" I asked, leaning on the banister. Helene idled at the house to visit with my mother after driving me back from my clinic.

"Well," she said, "I've already lifted the china and the silver, so I think I'll just sit right here and read my papers."

I smiled wanly at her, then trudged upstairs to the guestroom and set the tape on the dresser atop the stack of un-opened self-help books—*Hope and a Prayer; Healing of Soul, Healing of Body; Love, Medicine & Miracles; Fight For Your Life; Cancer as a Turning Point; Cancer: 50 Essential Things to Do;* and *If You're Afraid of the Dark*. After putting my cap on the nightstand, I patted some ointment on the irritated area of my scalp and crawled under the quilt.

I was jarred awake about an hour later by Helene's high-pitched laugh drifting through the screen of the guestroom window. She and my mother, as was their custom that week, were chatting in the Adirondack chairs on the second-floor deck.

I went downstairs and outside and climbed the steps. It was a mild autumn evening. "You girls behaving yourselves?" I asked, rubbing my eyes and stretching, the slatted floor creaking under my bare feet. There was a pulsating *tom-tom-tom* in my head.

My mother smiled at me, her eyes tired but warm in the dwindling light. She looked like a shrunken version of her wedding-photo self. No longer the vibrant woman who never seemed to stop, from her three-mile run at 5:30 each morning, to her work with troubled adolescents at her school, where her office doubled as the student lounge—did it still, now that she'd been, until this week, leaving early to drive me to radiation?—to her latest art project—silk-screening or mask making or etching—that sometimes took her into the wee hours of the morning; not the radiant woman who, on entering a gathering, made people smile in anticipation; who was never without a mate or one in pursuit. All of that, except work, on hold. For me.

"How about dinner, Helene?" my mother was saying, standing up and smoothing the front of her jeans; she had changed out of her work clothes. "Broccoli soup?"

Helene shook her head. I had not seen her eat anything other than a Yoplait Lite yogurt and, as she mentioned sometime that week, she took her principal meal—an ice cream sundae—at around midnight, leaving it ample time to digest through the late movies she watched into the early morning hours.

"What a mensch," my mother said as we stood on the front lawn watching the Lincoln Continental tear down the road. The crickets were trilling. The smell of fresh mown grass was in the air. She squeezed my shoulder. "She's really enjoying her time with you."

"Yeah," I said, turning toward the house. "She's actually sort of fun. Never would have guessed." I decided against telling her about Helene's unorthodox driving habits.

"And radiation went smoothly?" my mother asked.

"Walk in the park." I looked over at my mother, her drawn features, the deepened lines around her eyes. It was just as Luke said: she did appear worn down. She was struggling as much as I was, maybe more. And I never so much as acknowledged the healthy dinners, the food she scrupulously shopped for, the lunches she fixed for me every morning, along with whatever else I was missing.

All that, and she never asked for my thanks. She never suggested that I stay with my father or pointed out that he hadn't offered to take me in, knowing how that would hurt me, no matter my hostility toward her whenever I felt bad and scared and lonely. It was the same as ever: the easiest target— she'd always been, because she'd always been there for me.

"So, how about that soup?" my mother said. "Myra sent me the recipe." Myra and my mother had been best friends for years. She lived in Boston. She had sent me the scalp ointment.

"Sounds good." I inhaled sharply. I felt a lump in my throat. My eyes welled with tears. "Listen, Mom," I said. "I'm sorry for the way I've been acting. This is all just so awful."

"I know," she said, putting her arm around my shoulders. "I know."

"So?" Helene asked the next day when she picked me up. It was drizzling outside.

I had never really gone in for the self-help genre, I told her, my rain slicker squeaking against the leather of the passenger seat. "I guess I just like to figure things out on my own . . ."

We stopped at a red light. A broken-jointed umbrella lay in the road, the material flapping in the wind.

I wasn't telling Helene everything, how just before lunch I had gone as far as tearing off the plastic of the audiobook but then stopped myself.

It hadn't been an easy day. Each time I opened the front door and stepped onto the front stoop for a walk, the sky seemed to darken. I couldn't let myself lie down and close my eyes because then my thoughts would verge off into nightmarish eventualities, of knowing I was dying before I was ready to go.

Which was why I couldn't make myself listen to the tape: the fear that I'd hear something that would send me spiraling further downward. Instead, I set up my humus and sprouts sandwich on the desk in the study and stared out the window at the dreary day until it was time to get ready for my treatment.

"I want to tell you something," Helene said, pulling onto the highway. She cut into the left lane in front of a silver Corvette, chattily oblivious to the drone of an angry horn. When her husband left her and her two young boys, she was thirty-four and had never been alone. "Monogamy was not in that man's vocabulary—still isn't." She shook her head and shuddered in distaste. There was a truck ahead in the distance. The speedometer read seventy-five, eighty, eighty-five. Rain pelleted the windshield. She shifted her wipers to high. I tightened my seatbelt.

"But I was a mess," Helene was saying, taking a small sip of Diet Coke from a 7-Eleven Big Gulp plastic cup. She replaced the bottle in the holder and locked in behind the muddy truck, hitting her horn as she swerved around it. "Hey buster," she squealed out of her closed window in the direction of the truck cab. "Clogging the lane."

I clutched the dashboard and peered through the downpour at the wavering hues of autumn foliage. Helene was going on about her ex-husband refusing to pay her alimony or child support. The wet road hissed under her tires. "Can you imagine? I mean, me, a single mother, with no choice but to provide for my two—"

"Helene." I pointed at the steering wheel. I had stopped breathing. "Helene, two hands."

"Oops," she said. She clamped her other hand on the wheel. "Anyway . . ."

I was staring blindly at the slippery road, the wipers whisking away the rushing rain, my unease mounting. Who could say that we wouldn't skid into the barrier the next time? Or hydroplane into another vehicle? All my efforts to close myself off from what might disturb my fragile calm didn't mean I was any less vulnerable; all my pains to regulate my world to include only those who would be positive forces in my recovery gave me no more power over my circumstances. Nothing could erase the fact that I couldn't be sure of anything, couldn't trust that the car wouldn't end up a twisted mangle, couldn't know that I'd be okay. Seven weeks after the seizure had come out of nowhere, nothing seemed as improbable as it once might have been.

A siren wailed from afar.

"And so a co-worker of mine, she gave me a book. *Your Erroneous Zones.* I thought it was about sex." The car rocketed around the banked curve of the bridge leading to New Haven.

I gripped the side of the seat with my other hand.

"Can you imagine?" She looked over at me with a devilish grin.

"Helene," I heard myself saying, my voice rising. "Please. Eyes on the road." My heart ticked rapidly in my chest.

Sometimes you just need someone else to tell you, Helene was saying. She skirted around a Yugo wobbling along in front of us, pitching me sideways against the door.

"Helene," I shrieked, my hands flying to my head. "Helene, fucking slow down and get off at the next exit. I can't do this."

Helene complied. Her cheeks had turned an unearthly shade of pink.

"This is no good, Helene," I said once she had pulled into a vacant lot. The headlights from her car sheared through the thick fog. My whole body was shaking.

I gave her an ultimatum. If she kept her eyes on the road and drove the side streets to the clinic under thirty and then all the way home below sixty-five, I would listen to the tape. Something loosened in me as I spoke. For all of Helene's painstaking exertions to help, it was her very recklessness that had afforded me just what I needed: to be forced out of the protective shell into which I had retreated, to be driven to reassert control.

Helene kept her part of the deal, but not without considerable grumbling. "I'm doing this for you, but it's not natural," she said through clenched teeth, her arms and legs stiffened like a crash test dummy. "This baby was built to fly."

On Friday morning after breakfast, I slipped the tape into my mother's Walkman, setting the volume on low and positioning my finger on the OFF button. I made my way down the front steps and across the lawn. The sky had cleared; the air smelled damp and sweet.

I girded my body and pressed PLAY. As I neared the trail that led to the beach, I gritted my teeth and turned up the volume. *The path is difficult but it will lead to moments of great beauty* . . . That made sense. I thought of Luke and Cary coming through from the beginning, of my father's nightly phone calls and my mother's quiet constancy, of Helene, with all her quirks, doing what she could. And that *pain can be an agent for personal transformation*—I saw that too; maybe it had been already; it had to mean something that I'd made it this far; and the daily regimen that was starting to take form—that had to mean something too. Perhaps, indeed, *the person with the illness can be the great healer in the family, by showing everybody how to live ... despite an affliction.* That was it: this was my chance—not only to restore myself to health, but at last to bring peace between my parents.

Flushed with euphoria, I turned around and broke into a run, the first time I'd run since my initial radiation and chemotherapy treatments almost three weeks before, inhaling the briny scent of the sea, reveling in the piercing cries of the seagulls and the sparkling waters, feeling more alive than I had for days.

Five minutes later, I was dashing up the front steps, inside, and breathlessly cracking open *From Victim to Victor* to page one.

"They weren't half bad," I told Helene on the drive to the hospital that afternoon, a glistening afternoon, our last drive together. She was heading down to Baltimore to stay with

Luke and Cary for the weekend; my mother would pick me up after my treatment. "Part of it was actually sort of inspiring. I can definitely see how it might help some people."

I didn't tell Helene about the passage encouraging the use of laughter, laughter being a healing force—or, if possible, holding a sort of Joke Fest—as part of the fight for recovery, and how I found myself wondering if it was possible to engineer the outbreak of spontaneous laughter, much less throw a Joke Fest with myself as joke-maker and audience.

Nor did I share the recommendation to join a Wellness Community, a safe haven to reveal my fears, dreams, and fantasies with other Patients Active—patients, that is, actively fighting their disease—to build relationships so close and lasting that, as one Patient Active put it, she considered some members part of her family. Or how, having read that testimonial, I clapped the book closed, thinking of my conversation with Bob, grimacing at the prospect of a room filled with Bobs.

It wasn't that I was trying to spare Helene's feelings; I was not so noble. I just felt sad that she was leaving, sad enough not to say much at all, sad enough not to care that she had reverted to her usual eighty-five. Helene didn't say much either. Maybe she was sad too.

"Well, Helene . . ." The car idled in front of the clinic. I couldn't bring myself to say that I would miss her company. And that while she had on occasion tested my patience, she had also showed me that I could manage when things didn't break the way I expected them to, and that lesson was far more instructive than the platitudinous, if well-meaning, pronouncements in a self-help book.

I should have. I was just afraid I'd get weepy and I didn't want to go to my treatment looking like the guy with red-rimmed eyes. "Thanks for carting my sorry self back and forth," I said. "It meant a lot."

"Aw shucks." Helene rolled her eyes coquettishly, then blinked once, hard. "Anyhow," she said, lowering her sunglasses onto the bridge of her delicate nose, "I better get going. Gotta beat rush hour."

"As if rush hour would matter to the likes of you." I leaned over and gave her an awkward hug.

"You're going to be okay," she said, a tiny crack in her voice, as I was getting out of her car. She gunned her motor. "I just have a feeling."

And with a lurch and a screech, she was gone.

VIII

Around a bend rose cheers, shouts, clapping. I pedaled harder. In the foggy distance, runners were already finishing. I was an entire leg behind them.

Then I heard my name. "Lise!" "Lisa!" "GO, LISA!" My mother and Myra were waving, pumping their fists. A bolt of energy went through me.

While I was sick, those moments of pure exultation were that much more precious because I sensed I might not have too many more. I was wrong. But back then I hoarded them, put them on a high shelf of my memory to take down whenever they were needed.

One mild Sunday afternoon in the second week of October, in particular, when my mother appeared in the living room, her arms loaded with grocery bags and the two little pigtailed girls from the house next door hiding behind her legs. They wanted to watch me play the piano, she said.

By then, I'd undergone my second round of chemotherapy—though not without some trepidation as the treatment drew near. I discussed this with my great aunt Adele. "The idea of everything under the kitchen sink being pumped into my veins didn't faze me the first go-round, but I'm thinking I'll take your advice again," I said, before telling her about the lilac pants suit I was planning to sport, the same one I had favored during my darkest days in the law.

"That's marvelous," she said. "*Marvelous*, darling. And don't forget the lipstick."

Of course, it was the powerful anti-nausea medication, as well as Claire's agreement to seat me again in the alcove off the main ward, that gave rise to my upbeat report on the second treatment to Adele the next night.

Indeed, tagged as a patient with my hospital bracelet, rigged to the IV tubing, and yoked to the metal rack whenever I got tired of sitting still, I was no different from any of those whom I came to think of as the cancer people. And yet the notion of regarding the sick as a sect entirely foreign to me had taken hold ever since my first appointment with Dr. Quigley, and this extended to the hours outside the clinic.

By the week of my second round of chemotherapy, I was daily following a one-and-a-half-mile route from my mother's house, but I couldn't describe in any detail the clapboard houses overlooking the Sound or the old schoolhouse or the boats from the Yale Sailing Club bobbing in the water. Nor did I take much note of the riotous colors of autumn leaves or the seagulls wheeling above. I walked to recapture my body from the disease though I didn't think of it as such. I told myself I was in training.

At first I wormed along, eyes cast down on the asphalt, adding a little distance each time. As I grew stronger, I alternated walking and jogging between telephone poles and as I went along, I recited to myself the poems I was adding to my memory, repeating "And miles to go before I sleep/And miles to go before I sleep" over and over again so as to imbue my whole being with the message that it, too, had a long way to go before its final sleep. Likewise for Dylan Thomas' "Rage, rage against the dying of the light," which my mother suggested. And then Luke, who had studied English literature in college, challenged me to learn "Prufrock" during a conversation one night in late September.

"Already did," I said, popping a kale chip my mother had baked into my mouth. "And I loved some parts of it, like the line about measuring my life out in coffee spoons. But I never quite understood what it all meant. And it's pretty much gone."

"Try it again," she said. "You might hear something this time."

I didn't, at least not the first time I got through the 131 lines of "Prufrock" without referring to the copy of the poem I kept folded in my pocket, a Thursday evening, when my yoga class met down the road. I stood outside the door of the studio in the cool autumn air murmuring about sea girls wreathed with seaweed while the crickets trilled and the class ohmed their opening mantras.

With the dull glow from the soft lights on the polished hardwood floor, the gentle lute music, the smell of incense wafting across the small studio, and Chaula—Kilauha? Klaua? I could never remember her yogic name—our sylph-like snowy-haired leader gliding among us, I had little excuse not to "let it be, let it go," as Chaula gently urged in soothing tones.

I couldn't. I was too self-conscious to take off my baseball cap—the incision had healed, but there was still only stubble around the scar—even when the half-fish pose, which required resting the top of my head on the mat, crushed the bill. And I was so sure everyone was glancing sideways at me when I assumed the corpse position that I could never relax into it.

Then there was my concern that any or all of my fellow yoga mates—the dark-eyed brunette who invariably rushed in a few minutes late or the smallish bespectacled balding man with the knee-high gym socks or the large-boned matron with the leotard that was ever creeping upward—might wonder why I sat out certain postures: the headstand, for example.

Which was the reason I would book out of the studio immediately after the Namaste that ended the class. I told myself that it didn't seem yoga-like, socializing when I was supposed to be at one with myself, though I had never before practiced yoga, much less taken a yoga class. The truth was I didn't want to risk being asked about my cap or about anything else that would peg me as sick. I didn't want their solicitude. Or, worse, their pity.

Not to say I didn't enjoy the warrior pose, bending my left knee and lunging forward in the direction of the bare white wall, imagining myself as some composite of an Amazon and Wonder Woman. Or the way that yoga was loosening my neck and shoulders and improving my flexibility. But however strenuously I tried to "surrender to the moment," as Chaula intoned, I did not succeed.

It was the same with my attempts to meditate. During those days of frenzied purpose, I couldn't live in the moment; I was thinking only of what I should do next.

One morning in the first week of October, for instance. I was sitting in an upright chair with my eyes closed and the blinds drawn in my mother's bedroom, counting down from one hundred and my mind kept wandering to a clue in the crossword puzzle I hadn't finished; I did the one in the *Times* every morning to keep my mind agile. On ninety-three, Moose's tail brushed against my leg. After I had deposited her outside, closed the door, and started again, reaching eighty-nine, I heard a car horn sound when the word came to me— KLAXON—and then I found myself thinking about the empty boxes in the puzzle on the kitchen table and then to lunch and then what to wear to my radiation treatment and my bladder felt as if it were about to burst.

I must have knocked back at least two cups of green tea by then, though I never could get used to its cardboard flavor. That didn't matter. If nothing else, I could tell myself that its ingredients were better than the NutraSweet-laced bottles and bottles of Diet Snapple with which I used to caffeinate myself through fifteen-hour days at the office. As were the four to five twenty-four-ounce bottles of water I chugged every day: I kept track of my consumption on a chart taped to the refrigerator.

Processed sugar, on which I had depended for quick energy fixes, was out. So were my former mainstays butter and margarine; instead, I doctored salads and whole-grain bread with flax seed oil, which I heard improved brain function. When I learned that garlic might boost my immune system, I took to roasting several heads at a time, sometimes devouring so much in a single sitting that a powerful odor emanated from my pores for days.

"Did someone have Chinese for lunch?" Misty, Dr. Quigley's secretary, asked with a bemused smile one afternoon in the first week of October. She had waited for me at the radiation clinic after my treatment. I described the benefits of garlic. "Interesting," she said, and proceeded to tell me she had great news. My MRI was scheduled for the second of December. "Great," I said, as I felt the air go out of me.

Why it was great news I never learned, but the outlook of the radiation clinic personnel was so sunny that everything short of death, it seemed, was cause for celebration. Not that I minded. To be ushered in each day with a ringing "here she is" and to be told repeatedly how fabulous I looked did have its salubrious effects. So much so that in the middle of my six-week course of radiation, I asked Dr. Quigley if he might consider extending my treatments a few weeks longer. "That's a new one," he said, chuckling, before advising me that my brain by then would have absorbed all the zapping it could take.

In any event, awareness of the specific date of the MRI spurred me to greater exertions to calm my mind and avoid the panic that had overtaken me during the scan the day after my surgery. The next morning I interviewed a few hypnotists I had found in the yellow pages. One asked if I was allergic to dogs: she worked out of her apartment, she said, and had two "spirited" Chihuahuas. Another told me she was offering group lessons that featured exercises to free up "mind clutter" and "spring clean" the thoughts crowding my head while in the confines of the scanner.

I opted to improvise my own method of preparation. I threw an army blanket over the coffee table and inched my body underneath, cushioning my head on top of a thick pillow so that only a sliver of space remained, then flipped on a kitchen timer. For twenty-five, then thirty, then forty-five minutes each morning, I lay on my back, motionless. I don't know that I ever managed to clear my mind but that was okay. What mattered was that each time I did it, I felt that much more prepared.

I don't know the exact day I first lifted the top of the piano bench and discovered the pieces I'd been working on when I'd summarily stopped showing up at my lessons in ineffectual protest of my parents' divorce. But from then on, I practiced each morning, one time through, Joplin's *Maple Leaf Rag*, *The Entertainer*, and *Solace*, followed by Rachmaninoff's *Prelude in C-Sharp Minor*, and Beethoven's *Pathétique*, with the metronome set, in my first days of playing, at *adagio* speed, then at *andante*, then *allegro*.

At first, I practiced to fine-tune my hand-eye coordination but slowly, as my fingers regained their equilibrium on the keys and I managed to coax some measure of loveliness from the instrument, I turned off the metronome and luxuriated in the music.

Then came that early October afternoon when the two little girls from next door showed up in the living room with my mother.

"Any requests?" I asked.

They shook their heads, eyes wide. The smaller one disappeared further behind my mother's leg.

"Well, then, here you go," I said. And with my fingers tripping along the keys to the tune of *Maple Leaf Rag*, I choked back a surge of joy when I saw them, all scraped knees and socks around their ankles, bopping up and down, and my mother with a small smile on her face, and I was reminded—how could I have forgotten?—how much I loved performing, how I savored being recognized and appreciated.

That was one of the moments when I thanked my illness, when I loved my sickness. For simplifying my life to the essentials. For reminding me what made me feel alive.

RUN

I dismounted and jogged my bike through the waste-
land of wetsuits, abandoned bikes, strewn towels. In the thick
mist, the colors stood out like a pastel drawing. I set my bike
against a rack, replaced my helmet with a baseball cap, and
ran stiffly across the transition area, when someone shouted
my name.

In the distance was a lithe woman in her early fifties
with a streak of purple in her thatch of gray hair. She looked
familiar. Then I remembered. She was on the advisory board
of The Cove Center, an organization for children grieving the
death of a family member. She was gesturing at me and saying
something to a group of people standing near her.

"Hey Scoop," she called out as I started in their direction. "You gonna write about this one?" I'd interviewed her
after a road race benefitting The Center for an article I had
written in the local paper the year before.

"Run for The Cove," as the race was called, had been my
first story. I don't recall what possessed me to write about it,
except that Luke had a close friend whose young children par-
ticipated in its programs, only an editor agreeing to take it on
spec at the last moment. Nor at the time did I reflect whether
it would lead to anything or if I even wanted it to—it was a free
weekly that I regularly tossed after a cursory glance, a sort of
apology for a newspaper, I had snidely commented after my
mother suggested it as a natural fit for the piece.

Once the editor green-lighted the story, though, a fierce
sense of mission overtook me. For three thirteen-hour days,
through roughly a dozen drafts, I toiled on the six hundred
words I had been allotted, fueled by twice-daily trips to Star-
bucks and the terror of failing, again.

In the past nine years, I had already dead-ended as a
copyeditor; the job, involving documents translated from
Japanese into English required the use of spreadsheets, which

baffled me. I tried my hand at proof-reading a book on environmental degradation; the work was so mind-numbing that once having finished, I had no idea what the book was about. Of late I had been writing advertorials for a travel magazine; it paid well but the gigs were sporadic.

I still remember the peculiar thrill of flipping to page sixteen and seeing my byline in print. More vivid than that is the phone call from the director, thanking me as much for spreading the word on their work as for how I conveyed it. And that stirred in me a euphoria I had not experienced since I had been ill.

From then on, the way I saw the world changed. When I went to a shop to have a broken window pane replaced, I came away with an article about a gifted woodworker who had taught himself his trade by making renditions of antique pieces. Every store, every event, every person, offered the possibility of a story, one that involved a dream and a struggle. And somehow it came naturally, opening my Steno Pad, one question leading to another to another, each forging a stronger connection to my subject.

Not that it ever grew easy, the process of cobbling together those scribbled-down notes and quotes, of spackling them with hard facts and painting in sounds and smells and, finally, sanding down the whole to an even tone. Or that it ever became less daunting, the task of capturing that person's life or work, of dignifying it. Or that some of my pieces weren't duds.

Until the woman from The Cove Center identified me as a reporter to the people around her, however, it hadn't struck me that my little gig for the apology of a newspaper was anything more than a sideline hobby—I was a lawyer, I invariably found a way of idly mentioning when on assignment, though I had given only cursory thought to practicing since my resignation.

Now it hit me. After the foiled road trip, after the fruitless searching and the false starts, after hitting the restart button again and again, I had maybe, just maybe, found what I was looking for.

"Would you let me finish first," I called back to her, flashing a grin as I tried to pick up my pace. I couldn't. My legs felt like cement. But that was alright. I had been recognized. I had recognized myself.

And I'd gotten through the spell. Or the bonk. There are few things more exhilarating than experiencing the body's capacity to regenerate.

Except when it doesn't happen. Except when your body fails you. Not in any abstract way, like a diagnosis. When you watch it break down before your eyes. As, for example, in an eyelash.

At least that's what I thought it was. I flicked it off the *Times* crossword. I was scraping my bowl for the last of the oatmeal. Two more near an advertisement for Yankees World Series tickets in a shaft of harsh mid-October sunlight compelled a closer look. They were longer than ordinary eyelashes, more like half-inch commas.

I don't know exactly how much hair I had on the top of my head before I started losing it in earnest, and the reason was simple. Seeing my scarred, stubbly head only reminded me I was sick. Early on, I stopped looking at it.

Not to say I minded touching the affected area, especially after the scar had crusted over. There was something satisfying about sliding my fingers over my lightly textured pate and the thin seam running from the top of my skull to my right ear. Knowing the hair was coming back, that the scar was no longer raw and tender, made me feel as if I were healing as well.

Usually, though, I wore some kind of cap. Except for my crown, the rest of my shoulder-length hair remained. "So it looks like a monk's tonsure, only longer?" Luke asked after I'd described it to her on the phone one night in late September.

"Exactly." The prospect of looking like a medieval cleric didn't bother me. The hair was coming back; Dr. Quigley had said as much during our first appointment. And as long as I kept the area above my ears covered, there would be no way to tell, Luke added, before relaying Cary's offer to send me some vintage Baltimore Colts caps.

"Definitely," I said. "If I have to wear one for the time being, I might as well look like a badass in it."

Sure, there was the increasing itchiness I felt on my scalp in the last weeks of radiation. Otherwise, I was tolerating the treatments so well I figured I might not lose any hair at all. No shortage of energy or slowing of synapses, as was indicated for patients during the latter part of the six-week course of therapy: I continued my walks while reciting Dylan Thomas and T.S. Eliot. No loss of strength or coordination: I still lifted my five-pound weights each night, still practiced my Joplin rags at *allegro* speed, still did the *Times* crossword every morning, had even graduated from pencil to pen. Each day that passed, each week, I grew ever more convinced that I would be the one patient to beat the odds.

Then, that mid-October breakfast, the half-inch wisps appeared on the crossword puzzle. Followed that night by a scattering on the bottom of the bath as I stepped out of the shower. And when, the next morning, I saw a loose cluster on my pillow, it was clear that the statute of limitations on my good fortune was expiring.

To curb the sinking feeling in my chest, I quickly formulated a plan: beginning that morning, I would wear a cap at all times. I would no longer remove it to ventilate my scalp, not even while I was asleep. In that way I would create under my cap the humid environment conducive to germination and preservation rather than death and drop-off.

After only about eighteen hours engaged in this practice, I was awakened in the middle of the night by the sensation of insects scurrying across my scalp. The clock radio glowed 2:35. I turned on the bedside lamp. My cap was lying on its side on the floor near the opposite wall. I delicately placed my hand on my clammy pate. And gasped. Six or seven beetle-sized clumps of hair were sticking to my palm.

Other tactics were in order, more viable and, at the same time, more extreme. I began to refer to my hairs in the plural—I was losing hairs and not a head of hair—to distinguish the significance of each strand. I scared up a shower cap from the back of the linen closet, its moldy odor and lack of elasticity dating it back to the Reagan administration, and positioned it on my head with exquisite care. Deducing that the pressure of the water was washing away everything in its wake, I started taking baths instead of showers.

"Why are you yowling like that?" Luke asked one night in the middle of our conversation.

"I can't help it," I said, my hand clenching the phone, my body stiffened and bent over. "It's the only way to relieve the urge to scratch. It's been four days since this head has seen shampoo."

"Lise . . ." My sister let out a sigh. "It won't matter. Even if you tape the hair down to your head, it's still going to fall out." I could hear Cary erupt into a shout above the booming voice of a baseball announcer: "GOING . . . GOING . . . GONE!!!"

My mother stole into the study, the floorboards creaking under her clogs. She took a stack of bills and *Chicken Soup for the Surviving Soul* from her desk, squeezed my shoulder, and flicked on the table lamp on her way out.

The way radiation worked, Luke was saying, was by attacking rapidly dividing cells in the brain. That was why it was so effective against cancer cells. But there were also other cells that turned over rapidly in the same area, including hair cells. "And usually the hair comes out pretty quickly, in about a two- or three-week span, so—"

"But ultimately they'll be back. Dr. Quigley said they would."

"I think so. I haven't really looked at percentages. It should. And the good thing is it's just the top of your head, just the area where the radiation is aimed. You keep the rest. So when you wear a hat, it doesn't have to show."

"That's supposed to make me feel better? That I'll look like a monk? A female monk? A monkette? You said that yourself, remember?"

"Take it easy, Lise. It's not like it's a death sentence."

"Oops," I shot back. "We don't talk about that."

"Sorry," she said quickly. "Poor choice of words. All I'm saying is you can't do anything about it for now."

She was right, though I didn't renounce my quest to save the hairs until the end of October, about two weeks after the appearance of the first émigrés, when I inadvertently caught the top of my head in the bathroom mirror and saw Benjamin Franklin on a hundred-dollar bill.

I discovered in myself a newfound empathy for the men I had observed requesting Rogaine *sotto voce* at the pharmacy on Eightieth and Broadway and the junior partner who had marked himself for ridicule with black plugs springing from his shiny pate. Unlike theirs, my hairs were coming back in six months or a year, maybe, as I'd heard from a friend of my mother's early on, in a different color or texture, but they'd be back.

Oddly, it didn't occur to me that I might not be around once they resprouted. Or perhaps not so odd: the hair would work out one way or another. As for my survival, it was precisely as I put it to my sister: we didn't talk about it.

She did suggest that I ask Dr. Quigley about it at my follow-up appointment. Just to be sure, she said.

It was a bracing November afternoon, the first intimation of winter, and I had underdressed for the sole purpose of wearing the hunter-green blouse that favored my eyes, one of the radiation therapists once said.

But the chilly wind billowing through the raw silk as my

mother and I made our way from the parking lot did little to cool my anticipation of seeing Dr. Quigley—more than that, of showing him how stunningly I had skated through the six weeks of treatments and the ordeal as a whole.

This rush of overblown confidence wasn't unusual those days. I didn't know my prognosis, of course, and was content to remain in oblivion, but I knew it wasn't good; there was no other way to explain how readily Luke and Cary had agreed to keep me in the dark.

Still, however heavily I armored myself in denial, I was still reading a portent into the kitchen clock that stopped ticking and the cancer-fighting blueberries my mother brought home that were rotting from the bottom up. I was still regularly waking up in the middle of the night, clutching my mattress, to keep myself from falling through blackness.

At times, though, the dire nature of my condition had an opposite effect. There were those moments when a light of energy would shimmer through me as I flew through the last mile of my route or my fingers would trip through all my piano pieces without so much as a missed key, and I'd grow convinced that this kind of adversity had come to me for a reason, that I was one of the chosen few capable of handling it.

It went further than that. The longer I contemplated the near-certain death Christiane's rescue had forestalled, as well as the ease with which I'd tolerated my treatments, the more fervently I believed that there was something preordained about the miraculous recovery I would make. Even the fact that it was a brain tumor of the highest grade of malignancy, for the sheer terror it inspired, had a certain perverse glamour to it.

All this I kept to myself. It might undermine the impossible feat I would, contrary to all expectations, achieve. Not to mention the risk that, by disclosing my special powers, I could lose them.

It was in that frame of mind that I casually asked Dr. Quigley when I might expect my hairs back. He had been chatting with my mother, something about his youngest son's Harry Potter costume on Halloween.

It was the first I'd heard he had children and was, I assumed, married. I was too preoccupied to react. My father had just then walked in and I had to endure the ritual of greetings and a short discussion about the unseasonably cold weather.

I barely heard Dr. Quigley remark that there was only a forty percent chance they would come back. I was more concentrated on his physique. He appeared softer and thicker than the other two times I'd seen him. His wry smile rankled as well; it seemed grotesquely inappropriate, and with no small measure of self-control, I resisted the impulse to ask what was so funny or whether his face was just set in that idiot grin.

And that my mother and father said nothing, just sat there stone-faced, even as I appealed to them to back me up, to verify that Dr. Quigley had in fact asserted that the hair loss would not be permanent—that was no matter: I could handle it myself. I wasn't a patient passively acquiescing to her doctor's pronouncements. I was a courtroom lawyer, firing questions, ever more specific, backing the defendant into the response I was seeking—that he couldn't state beyond a reasonable doubt that the hairs wouldn't grow back, that they might not be the same, but they would still, eventually, reappear.

Until his voice rose up, deep, decisive, and unequivocal, seeming to echo off the cold, hard linoleum and concrete-block walls, silencing my increasingly desperate pleas—"did you not say?" .... didn't you tell me?" . . .—"Look, it'll never be the same. It's not coming back completely, ever. Best-case scenario, it'll be patchy."

"And you just conveniently forgot to mention this when we first met?" I asked, still in indignant lawyer mode, not yet taking in his words, poised to ask whether his alleged National Spelling Bee championship was a half-truth as well.

"I'm sorry," he said.

I felt hot, dizzy, deflated. There was a ringing sound in my ears. I fixed my eyes on the blood-pressure monitor on the side wall. As everyone stood, I pulled myself up, wobbled across the room, waved perfunctorily in his direction, then at Misty just outside, her mouth in a rictus of false cheer.

The three of us trudged down the halls and into the biting autumn air, the sunlight already beginning its cruel early fade, past the hurrying white-jacketed interns, our feet crunching on the dead leaves through the sparse patch of grass in front of the clinic.

Head down, I let the sting of humiliation propel me forward, for wearing that blouse for such a putz as Dr. Quigley, for investing in him the power to reassure me that my hairs would return and, more than anything, for being so delusional as to suppose I was different from anyone else.

By the time we reached the parking lot, tears were streaming down my cheeks. I wiped them away. There was a smear of lipstick across the cracked skin on my knuckles. Everything was falling apart.

My mother put her hand on one of my slumped shoulders; I wriggled away. "No," I said. "Please. Just let me alone."

"Kiddo," my father said. "I forgot—this is from Marjy." He handed me a red card made of construction paper. "She said to tell you she misses you."

I took the card and waved him away. "Yeah, tell her me too," I said in a threadbare voice not my own. One look at Marjy's crooked handwriting and the painstakingly drawn misshapen hearts and I felt an ache spreading inside, an ache of longing for the way I used to pop in on Marjy after work and have running races with her up and down the twelfth-floor hallway of Christiane's apartment, an ache for the way my life had been. "I'll call you tonight."

There was nothing he could do, nothing I could do. The strategies I had developed to manage most effects of the treatments—my focus on acting as if I were well, the regimen from which I rarely strayed—were unavailing for hair loss. No matter how many miles I walked or how many cups of green tea I drank each day, no matter how deeply I meditated under the coffee table, the hairs might not come back. And even if they did, a hat for the rest of my life. There was no Kleenex in the glove compartment, just a dirty cloth for when the window fogged up, so I used the sleeve of my corduroy jacket to wipe my nose.

"It could be worse," my mother said, her eyes set on the road. She was speaking evenly, but the little muscle near her nose was twitching. "You do look good in hats."

I sniffled. I didn't want to use a hat as some makeshift measure; I wanted to figure out a way to save the hairs. I wanted to beat the odds.

"What an asshole," Luke said on the phone that night. "I can't believe he was fucking grinning when he told you. But it's partly my fault. I probably should have looked into it. But Lise —it's just hair. It doesn't really have to do with your health."

"I know," I said as a jagged pain shot through my temple. I was stretched out on the couch in the darkened study, sapped of emotion, the remote lying loosely in my hand. I had drifted from program to program for the rest of the afternoon and evening. Every channel, it seemed, was airing shampoo commercials.

"Lise?" My sister sounded concerned. I heard my mother in the kitchen. She'd been on her cell phone talking to her friend Myra since I had come in for a glass of water about twenty minutes before. Was she worried too?

"I'm here," I said. "And you're right, it has nothing to do with my health." I watched a character mindlessly run her

116

fingers through the swarm of her long honey-brown hair, then glanced at Marjy's card beside me—I MISS YOU, LEELEE!!!! it read—again feeling the knot in my throat, the tears again starting in my eyes. I kept thinking of Dr. Afshari. I'd thought about her from time to time since my week at the hospital but had never before considered contacting her.

One of my mother's bobby pins skidded into the study. Moose followed in hot pursuit.

"Plus it'll be winter soon and no one will think twice about me wearing a hat all the time," I added, deciding against calling Dr. Afshari. I could deal with this on my own. Besides, Luke was right. There was no reason to get so unglued over something cosmetic. My life was what mattered.

And yet I was losing it. The prospect of having, at best, patches of hair on my head for whatever time I had left preyed on some of my deepest insecurities—about my looks, my desirability. I hadn't thought much about being with anyone since the surgery. Then again, I hadn't thrown out the condoms Dotie had slipped me in the hospital room.

In part I sensed Jake would wait. After a hiatus of a month or so, he'd been phoning again and I'd answered once or twice, but I never let the conversations wander, just told him I wasn't up to talking too long. More than that, I didn't want to get sidetracked from the march toward getting better with any kind of emotional distraction.

That was what I told myself anyway. Really, I felt disfigured by the illness, couldn't imagine how I could ever again feel attractive not just to Jake, but to anyone, with my brain tumor and freakish-looking scalp. And beyond all that, Luke was right: it wasn't a matter of life or death.

Which was why I didn't tell my father much when he rang earlier to check up on me. I didn't want to sound as if I were feeling sorry for myself. But that couldn't quiet a new and sickening reality: it wasn't really about the hair, but the loss of control it signified—that whatever plan I devised, the force of the disease might make it irrelevant, that whatever I did, I might not survive.

"You there, Lise?" my sister was asking.

"Yeah," I said, my voice scrabbly. The shooting pain had dulled. "Just thinking." I rubbed my eyes. "Mom and I are going hat shopping." The two Cary had sent a few weeks earlier no longer covered the growing swath above my ears. "Just no turbans and scarves. Too cancer-y."

"Or wigs," my sister said. "Although you could be a blonde. A dumb blonde. Finally, a dumb blonde in the family."

"Not in this life," I said.

She was silent.

"No wigs," I said quickly. "Or burqas. Or helmets. That would make it too obvious. Maybe a beret?"

"Yeah, a beret. You'd look great in one, Lise."

I lingered on the couch after hanging up with Luke, imagining myself in a beret, feeling increasingly sanguine. Maybe this setback would access another side of myself, the side I'd been seeking to discover after I left the law. The carefree, insouciant side; the side that didn't make lists or charts, that didn't strategize or plan, that just lived.

It was meant to be, I told myself, as I trudged up the stairs, an opportunity for reinvention, I decided, as I got under the covers and removed my cap. And even if it wasn't, I would figure it out, I resolved when I woke up the next morning after a deep dreamless sleep, a bright gleaming morning.

On my way to the kitchen, I caught my reflection in the living-room mirror. Something about my face seemed off. I turned the bill of my cap around to the back of my head and drew closer. The outside of my right eyebrow had begun to disappear.

It was doubtless only a matter of days before the entire brow would be gone, and likely the other one as well, before I would have to pencil in arcs above my eyes each day. Somehow the idea of presenting a mask-like face to the world was too much to bear.

I lowered the shades and sat down hard in the patchwork chair, cupping my head in my hands and hardly breathing.

II

I passed the two-mile marker. Two miles to go. Two miles. What were two miles? Eight laps around a standard track. Fifteen, sixteen minutes. And except for a small rise or two it was flat. I'd gone over the course on my bike the day before.

The rain had become a light mist; the sun peeked through the clouds. There was a coolness in the air. An expanse of manicured lawns fronted cream-colored mansions on one side and calm waters on the other. Perfect.

I turned onto a side road, accelerating past another runner on the puddled road. I was getting stronger, my breathing slow and even, my movements fluid, making up the time I had lost swimming and biking. Like a pitcher's fastball approaching 100 mph deep into a game. *He's found his groove*, the announcer would say. *Just letting it fly.* I was the running equivalent. I concentrated on keeping my shoulders relaxed, my arms and legs in sync.

As my confidence grew, my heart opened. I became the loathsome cheerleader. "We're almost there," I called back to a guy as I breezed past him. "Hang in there."

This was why I loved running above all. It was on the roads where I first forged my identity within our family, where I learned that an A on my report card wasn't the only way to excel and, more than anything, that I could suffer pain and doubt and still function. And still now, where no worry loomed about my head being dunked in the deep of the Sound or my tires skidding on the slippery road.

Nothing could touch me as I powered around a bend in the road, not even the sense of doom that had shadowed me as time stretched and lengthened since my diagnosis, the sense that, despite all those years I'd been well, despite the firmness of the ground beneath me, something else might be stirring up trouble inside, something that out of nowhere could sweep my feet out from under me.

Which probably went a long way in explaining why I preferred trysts and short-term relationships to anything longer in the past nine years. "I'm not worth the trouble," I told Jake on the phone six months or so after I had completed my treatments. It gnawed at me, how he kept trying, given the way I had alienated him. That was part of it.

But I also knew I didn't want to settle for someone just to settle. Not with him.

Not with anyone, it turned out. My hair had grown back almost fully but I still saw myself as blighted, damaged goods, a ticking time bomb. And then, after a while, I grew habituated to being alone. Maybe that would change at some point; I didn't know.

Whatever the case, it only followed, it occurred to me later, that the triathlon, with its long hours of solitary training, so naturally suited me. Not to mention my work as a reporter, which involved a week or two of intense, but transitory, intimacy.

Another turn, another road, another sightline of the glistening waterfront, and my legs showing no signs of their earlier heaviness, my breathing still easy. That was the other side of it. The magnificent biological machine that was my body.

And that was my celebration: that I could overcome, that I could recover, recover my bearings, recover my strength, my spirit. That I could persevere. Even in something as inconsequential as a sprint triathlon in a small corner of the world, that meant something.

It wasn't a sign of invincibility. Not at all. Or courage; I'd been tagged with that word and it made me cringe. It wasn't courage. It was something primitive, an inability to let go, a selfish fear of depriving the world of myself.

And even that impulse presupposed a control over my circumstances. I had none. What had I done, after all, except follow doctors' orders and show up at every treatment? What had I done in those five months in 1998, apart from getting lucky? A little to the left of my brain and it would have been a different story. And since then, what had I done but muddle on?

Which was why my T-shirt did not proclaim TEN-YEAR BRAIN CANCER SURVIVOR. And also why I needed to cross the finish line. I needed a medal, even a cheap, tinny one, something that would mark not just that I was still alive but, what seemed far more momentous, had endured.

Just then I saw it: a NO OUTLET sign and beyond a stretch of marsh, a dock bobbing on the water. And grew aware it was silent. The route was twisty and convoluted, like a map that had been crumpled and then smoothed out. The street names were confusing too, overlapping each other, changing from Place to Road to Lane, as if on a whim—I knew that from having reconnoitered the course the afternoon before.

But then the sun had been shining. There had been arrows chalked onto the road. Now the rain had washed them away.

Nadir: The lowest point. Or points.

Dr. North had defined the word as it applied to white-cell counts. As had Dr. Moshe Aronson, Dr. North's fellow. And Luke, repeatedly. No cause for concern, they all insisted. To be expected. Just wait it out.

On the mid-November morning I wormed along, head down, on my walking route, I was beyond concerned. I was beyond anxious or panicked. By then I felt like the carpet of dead leaves crunching under my feet—trampled, withered, decomposing.

Eight days earlier, on the morning of my third round of chemotherapy, a whisper of a man with thinning hair in a white lab coat haltingly approached Luke and me. We were sitting side by side in the alcove off the main oncology ward, the same area I'd occupied during my first two rounds. Luke had traveled by train from Baltimore the previous night to keep me company.

"Ms. Reisman?" he said, his gloomy eyes flitting between my sister and me. The identification tag hanging from his scrawny neck read DR. MOSHE ARONSON. I'd been working on the *Times* crossword. Luke had that week's New Yorker on her lap, and her cell phone and beeper on the tray table to give my mother updates and to call my father, who had promised to walk over from the law school during the three-hour treatment. We had been chuckling about the saleswoman at the millinery shop who had stoutly maintained that cowboy hats were coming back.

"That would be me," I said to Dr. Aronson, still grinning as I waved my hand, the Band-Aid that Claire had applied to the back of my hand after drawing my blood flapping free.

Curiously the apprehension I'd felt before my first two rounds of chemotherapy had all but dissipated. Indeed, since my radiation treatments had ended, I'd found myself counting the days until the next round of chemotherapy, mostly out of my growing concern that the various measures I had been taking to complement the treatments were just that—complements, insufficient in and of themselves to stop the cancer cells from spreading. Hadn't my bald pate proven as much?

There was something else: I felt stronger in the ward, less susceptible to my fear of identifying with the patients there. Or perhaps I'd just trained my eyes to cut away from the woman with the sunken eyes and bloated stomach who had earlier shuffled into the alcove to get water from the tank. "Ready to go?"

"I'm sorry," he said in an adenoidal tone that sounded

Israeli. He was holding a sheet of paper and looking pained. "We can't go ahead. You have to come back."

"No problem." I checked my watch. 10:05. "What time?"

"No," he said. The paper quivered in his hands. From the main ward, Sally Jessy Raphael scolded away on the television over the thrum of activity: "Now just one moment, buster. . ."

"What?" I asked.

"The counts." He thrust the paper at me. "They're too low."

It was a chart with columns of letters and numbers titled CBC WITH DIFFERENTIAL. Two numbers were circled in pen. "What does this mean," I said, a queasiness going through me. "Luke?"

My sister studied the chart, her eyes betraying nothing. She couldn't help me. She was a doctor, naturally, but oncology wasn't her specialty; it was hardly within her province to dispute Dr. Aronson's decision. Besides, Luke, unlike me, wasn't one for confrontation. I remained the athlete, the aggressor; she, the accommodating bookworm. Which was why, though she was my older sister, I'd never counted on her to protect me. Until I got sick.

Until that moment.

"Luke," I said, opening my eyes wide at her. "Luke, please. What's going on?"

My sister handed the chart back to Dr. Aronson. "Maybe if you could explain to us how—"

Claire hurried back into the alcove, wheeling the IV rack with the saline pouch and the bottles of Zofran and BCNU. Dr. Aronson shook his head at her. She stopped short by the water tank, her blue eyes freezing, her freckled face registering the news.

I clapped my hand on top of my hat. "Jesus, motherfu—"

"Lise, calm down," my sister said quietly.

123

I closed my eyes and tried to compose myself. There was a reek of disinfectant in the air. I didn't want this guy for my doctor, making the decisions, this puny guy who looked like he compulsively bit his nails and then studied them for further gnawing. "Does Dr. North know about this?" Dr. Aronson seemed to shrink back. "Where is she? Can we talk to her?"

Claire told me she was at a conference in California for the week.

"Holy fuck," I said under my breath, shaking my head, feeling the knees of my jeans bouncing up and down. How could Dr. North be in California? And how could it escape this noodle of a man that a delay was out of the question, that this treatment was all I had left, was all that was keeping the cancer at bay?

"Lise," my sister said. "Take it easy."

Dr. Aronson tugged at his stethoscope.

"At least can you tell me what I'm doing wrong? What am I doing wrong? What can I do to boost the whites?" Someone in the main ward laughed, a whinnying joyless laugh. I needed to get out of there.

Dr. Aronson stumbled in his efforts to answer, but I waved him off. "Forget it," I said, tossing the crossword puzzle in my bag, reaching for my coat, and standing up.

Luke stayed put. Of course she would, I thought, head down, face burning, as I made for the hall. Same as ever.

I trudged past the old schoolhouse, the second beach, remembering how I'd tagged a couple feet behind Luke on our way to the car eight days earlier, feeling dejected and increasingly fragile, taking small, careful steps, as though any abrupt movement might loose more cells.

First, the hair, now this; the same walk back to the parking lot, the same sense that everything was hurtling out of control. But now the hair seemed like a cruel tease. This was my life. The longer I went without chemotherapy, the more tumor cells could spread.

"Lise," my sister said, looking back as she clicked the remote and reached for the door handle. Her eyes were hidden behind her sunglasses. "Relax."

I couldn't stand when she told me to relax; it only made me more riled.

"OHM," I said in a loud voice as I slid into the passenger seat, the petty, moody teenager all over again. "OHM."

"Jesus," I heard her say under her breath. She studied the instrument panel and awkwardly pried back the gear shift. "Do you want me to explain this to you or not?"

"I'd much rather continue our discussion on the startling resurrection of cowboy hats," I said. "Because all I know is this sucks."

"It does, but I don't think it's as bad as it seems." She looked over to make sure I had fastened my seatbelt. She had my father's nostrils, most strikingly in the way they flared when she was making a point. She also had his rationality, particularly in the midst of a crisis. "Basically, it's the same deal as the hair loss. Tumor cells rapidly divide. That's why chemotherapy works, it's aimed at rapidly dividing cells."

A siren shrieked. An ambulance, its lights flashing, raced by.

"The problem is that chemotherapy isn't refined enough to target only tumor cells," my sister continued, ignoring the commotion. She peered into the rearview mirror and tentatively backed out of the parking space. "Other cells rapidly divide, normal cells, and they get hit as well. Including hair cells. Including white blood cells. And—"

"That's all well and good," I spat out. I couldn't stand how calm she was. "But you come all the way up here to help me. To help. And all you could do was just goddamn nod your head. It's like always." I punched the dashboard; it stung my fist. "You're a doctor, a GODDAMN FUCKING DOCTOR." I

125

was shouting. It felt good to shout. "The least you could have done was fought for me, or at least challenged him. You're a doctor and nothing has changed. As meek and mousy as ever. What, were you afraid you might offend him? Afraid of offending a puddle for being a puddle? Why'd you come up at all?" I rubbed my hand.

"At this moment I honestly couldn't tell you," my sister said. She checked each side for oncoming cars and turned onto the street. "Anyhow, do you want me to go on or not?"

We stopped at a red light. She drummed her fingers on the steering wheel. I stared out the window in sullen silence at two guys in scrubs making their way back to the hospital. They were holding Dunkin' Donuts coffee cups and laughing. "You're here," I said. I knew I was being impossible but I didn't care. I didn't care about anything. "You might as well."

"Okay," she said, shifting into first gear. "Here's the deal. White blood cells live in your bone marrow. Actually, according to Dr. Aronson"—Luke had spoken with him for a few minutes while I fumed in the hall—"what we're concerned with is a certain type of white cell, neutrophils."

"Neutro-phil?" I asked, adjusting the sun visor downward to block the late-morning glare. "What the hell does that mean? Friend to neither? No-one? Nothing?"

"Literally, I guess." She pulled onto the highway. "It's your body's main defense against bacteria. Bacteria that can cause infections." Neutrophils differ from other white blood cells insofar as they constitute the front line, she said; millions of neutrophils are the first to arrive at the site of an infection and destroy the bacteria. The chemotherapy, in addition to wiping out cancer cells, gradually decreases the number of neutrophils.

A bus with black-tinted windows, MOHEGAN SUN CASINO emblazoned on its side, shot by. I felt a sudden nostalgia for Helen's reckless driving. How I wished that was still my greatest concern.

"At a certain point in a given cycle—yours is five weeks—the neutrophils hit a nadir," Luke was saying. "Which is good because we know a lot of cells are being destroyed, including tumor cells." She was pressing her lips together. Was she on edge? I couldn't tell. "And which is bad because it means you can't have another treatment until your neutrophil count is higher, until, in other words, your immune system is stronger."

"Okay," I said, appraising myself in the visor mirror. I looked fine. The chronic dark circles under my eyes appeared lighter. My skin was pale but clear; the shoulder-length hair under my hat looked normal enough. Even my right eyebrow seemed barely changed. A well-preserved façade with a rotting interior. "So I have to get the counts up. How? How can we get them to come back?"

"I don't really know," Luke said. "I think you just have to wait."

I flipped the visor back up and squinted into the indifferent November sun. "What I don't get is my cycle is five weeks. It's over. Doesn't that mean that the tumor cells have more time to spread, even as we speak?" An image crossed my mind of insects chomping their way through my brain, eroding my memory, my sight, my motor functions. I squeezed my eyes shut. "What's the worst thing that could happen if we just went ahead and did the treatment? Because I'd do it. I don't care. I'd just be more prone to infection, right? So I'd be more careful. I wouldn't go out. I could be the Girl in the Plastic Bubble."

"Lise, that's ridiculous. Your nadir is just later than normal."

"Ugh." It sounded as if we were discussing whether I was pregnant. Pregnant. The idea of having children was for me something far off and undefined, but now, it seemed, it was entirely out of the picture. Because here I was, yearning for chemicals to be pumped into my body, chemicals that would pollute my body, that would contaminate whatever might grow inside me. I felt like pounding the windshield, breaking it into little pieces. I felt like pounding my head against the dashboard, over and over, to stop the spreading.

"You just have to wait," Luke was saying. "They'll come back up. They will." She switched on the blinker, looked into the rearview mirror, and crossed into the slow lane. "Anyway, you better call Dad so he doesn't show up. Cell phone's in the front pocket of my bag."

My father picked up on the first ring. "How's it going, kiddo?" His voice had an unnatural cheeriness. "When should I stop by?"

"No treatment," I said, watching a broken light from the sign of a car dealership flicker on and off. I suddenly felt drained. "Something about low blood counts. Luke'll call you when we get back to the house," I said, my voice hollow.

"I'm sorry, kid." I thought I heard him sigh.

"Yeah. Me too."

We didn't do much for the rest of the day. Luke rang my father, read *The New Yorker*, then the novel *Cold Mountain* and some medical journals, fielded a call from Cary, updated my mother. I napped fitfully on the sofa. Luke fixed me a slice of multi-grain bread with flax seed oil. We tried to play duets on the piano, the way we used to each time we visited my mother, but I could never sight-read as quickly as she could and soon gave up and walked away. In the late afternoon, she asked if I wanted to go down to the water. "I don't feel like it," I said, looking outside. It was already dusk.

Dusk. Gloom. I didn't feel like doing anything. My head felt numb, except for a tingling sensation whenever I remembered I hadn't gotten my treatment.

"Don't worry, Lise," Luke said that evening, holding her overnight bag. She was going back to Baltimore that evening, as planned. My mother was taking her to the train station.

"Relax. They'll come back up."

My mother nodded emphatically, as if to underscore my sister's words. But she was jingling her keys nervously in one hand.

They stood in the vestibule, nodding. Except for their dark-brown hair and eyes and matching pea coats, they didn't look anything alike, my mother, tall and olive-complected, my sister, fair-skinned and of medium height.

But they were both nodding. It worried me, how much they were nodding.

I plodded by the pocket-sized post office, where I usually turned around, and kept going. There was nothing to rush home for, I reasoned, recalling, with a quickening of anger and irritation, Dr. Aronson's appeal for patience following a blood test at a local lab two days after the aborted round of chemotherapy; it showed my blood counts had sunk even lower.

"Sure, your nadir is late," Luke said during our nightly call that evening after I had bullied Dr. Aronson into admitting that it usually occurred in the third week of the cycle. "But it's still no cause to be alarmed."

"Imagine the bone marrow as a machine producing white-blood cells," Cary said three days later when an exasperated-sounding Luke passed the phone to him. I'd had a third blood test and the number of neutrophils had again dropped. "Yes, the chemotherapy shuts off the machine and its capacity to produce cells but it doesn't destroy the basic workings of the machine. Eventually it'll fire up again."

But I couldn't accept their bidding—to sit there, patiently—passively—waiting. There had to be some way. Each day that passed without treatment, each hour, more cancer cells could spread.

Fifty yards down the street from the post office, I turned right, passing a brick-red house with a spacious porch. It looked familiar. That was when it struck me: I was nearing my younger sister Pip's group home.

All at once, I felt slightly woozy. It might have been the length of the walk or a twinge of uneasiness about seeing Pip after so much time. More likely, it was the Chinese tea I had taken with breakfast, so foul-smelling that I'd had to plug my nose each time I raised the cup to my mouth.

The day before, I had caught the train for the hour-long ride to Stamford to meet with Dr. Xiu-Ju Chang, a specialist in Chinese medicine, world-renowned, according to a friend of mine who moonlighted at the computer support desk at my law firm.

When she wasn't typing or writing, the friend was poring over the daily horoscope; she also wore a crystal necklace—fluorite, she told me—to ward off electromagnetic stress from the computer. Once I would have peremptorily discounted any New Age-related advice from her. No longer. I could also disregard the driving rain that blurred the windows of the Metro-North train as well as the two shining Mercedes in Dr. Chang's garage when my taxi pulled up to his sprawling home.

Such was the force of my conviction that a resort to Eastern medicine, to the earliest and most organic form of healing, would signal the turning point in my exertions to raise the number of neutrophils and set my recovery back on course.

"Please," he said, gesturing toward a leather-upholstered couch in his wood-paneled basement office. He was small and stooped over with a soft, wrinkled face. He parked himself behind a large oak desk, his white lab coat bunching up over his small paunch. The desk was heavily varnished and bare.

"Okay," I said. "This is what's wrong." I wasn't used to specifying what was wrong but this was hardly the time to be posturing as healthy. "I have a brain tumor." It felt strange to say it, as if I were talking about my troubled child. Also I seldom voiced the words "brain tumor" or "brain cancer": to my ears those words had a ring of obscenity to them. Instead I primly referred to it as "my condition."

I tapped the right side of my hat. "I need chemotherapy. To get chemotherapy, I need a way to boost—increase—my white-cell count. My neutrophil level, specifically."

"Hm. White cell," he said. He took a square pad out of the top drawer, set it on the desk, and noted something in Chinese characters. Behind him loomed a hulking cabinet with hundreds of tiny drawers.

"Neutrophils." A dryer hummed and knocked in the next room.

"Neutrophils," he repeated, nodding, as he made his way around the desk and across the carpet and perched himself beside me on the couch. The leather squeaked. "Closer," he said, motioning with his hand toward him.

I moved closer.

He pulled down my eyelids. "Hm," he said. "Hm." He smelled like licorice. "Hand," he said.

I extended my right hand to him. There was a brown mole near his nose. He turned my hand over and kneaded my palm deeply with two fingers, tilting his head upward. It felt good. I made a mental note to look into massage therapists when I got back.

I gazed past his close-cropped peppery hair in the direction of the rain-splotched basement window, willing him to give me the answer I needed. "Ah," he said, his eyes closed. "Aha."

Heels clicked on the floor upstairs.

"What?"

"Worry too much," he said. "Worry too much."

Of course I worried. But I hadn't traveled all the way to Stamford in a heavy downpour to hear the obvious. "Yeah, I worry," I said, sinking back into the cushions. My head was sweltering under my hat. "But what about the neutrophils?"

"Hm," he said, nodding. "Neutrophil." He narrowed his eyes. "Yes." He got up and shuffled toward the cabinet.

Perhaps I should have mulled over the wisdom of scribbling out a $250 check to Dr. Chang for the Ziploc bag of herbs he handed me from one of the tiny drawers. I didn't. I barely heard him giving me directions on how, how much, and how often, before collecting my umbrella and asking him if I could use the telephone to call a taxi to the train station. Desperation had blurred the boundary between viable remedy and dubious curative alternative.

I had already ordered shark cartilage pills from a natural health remedy web site and popped three or four before each meal. I had doubled my intake of soy and green tea and had started taking astragalus, a tonic herb, which, the pony-tailed guy at the local health food store drawled, would "amp up the whites." When his colleague, a sad-eyed, slope-shouldered woman, produced an article showing shiitake mushrooms stimulated white-cell function, I prevailed on my mother to incorporate them into every meal.

I had engaged in visual imagery under the coffee table, laboring to summon images of my bone marrow grunting and wheezing back into white-cell production. I had drawn intricate pictures of multiplying neutrophils—two, then four, then eight, and so on—until I had worn the white crayon down to a nub. For its rejuvenating properties, I had sampled wheatgrass juice which tasted as if I were drinking my mother's backyard.

There was virtually nothing I wouldn't try. And yet, following my fourth trip to the hospital later that afternoon, a week after my third round of chemotherapy had been postponed, the neutrophil count had dropped again.

Except for the wheelchair ramp and the gravel lot on one side, the neat one-story residential structure was indistinguishable from the other houses that lined the street. In the front was the van that transported the residents to their day program and their weekly visits to the mall.

There were three cars in the lot but five minutes after I pressed the doorbell, I was still waiting. I had already pulled my cap over my right eyebrow, which had shrunk a bit more, rapped on the door a few times, and surveyed the immediate area before climbing down behind the bushes and peering inside the front windows.

The blinds were drawn. I contemplated trying to let myself in but something stopped me. For one thing, I hadn't called ahead. More than that, I wasn't exactly a regular: there often had been months between my visits, and those visits, while on various breaks from school, or later, during slow patches at work, were more obligatory than anything.

That was when it hit me. There was no time for obligatory visits when everything I did had to be channeled into increasing the number of neutrophils. Pip couldn't help me, didn't even know who I was, had never said a word, much less my name. That hadn't stopped me from seeing her before, of course. She was my younger sister and however inaccessible she was, that biological connection was there.

And that in itself was another reason to avoid seeing her: the alarming probability that like her, no matter what happened, I'd always be damaged; I'd always be compromised. There was no way I had it in me to face that just then.

As I was turning back toward the road, the screen door swung open. A large-boned woman with short-cropped hair and gentle brown eyes appeared, apologizing—"helping Dorothy in the bathroom," she said breathlessly—and beckoning me in. Her T-shirt read DON'T MESS WITH BARBARA. "Good to see you, Lisa," she said warmly, almost as if she'd been expecting me.

I wondered if she knew. My father visited Pip nearly every week—had ever since he'd had her moved from a facility in New Jersey eight years earlier. Then again, I couldn't imagine him confiding in Barbara. He was polite enough to the staff but that was as far as it went. I pulled my cap more tightly over my head.

"Everyone!" Barbara called out, bustling into the living room. "Debbie's sister is here!"

The only response was the high-pitched voice of the Pillsbury Doughboy from the wide-screen color television.

I set my leaf-caked running shoes next to a plastic pumpkin in the foyer, taking in the familiar diaper smell, and scanned the living room. There was Sharon, a tiny wizened sixty-year-old with Down's syndrome, smiling and humming to herself at the end of the long couch closest to the television. And Dorothy, around forty, with rough-hewn features and a shock of black hair, skittering in from the bathroom on the hall off the living room, dark eyes darting fiercely around, and upon seeing who had come in, making a beeline for her bedroom. Heavy-lidded James, who had been rocking on the easy chair against the back wall, got up and stalked in my direction, studied me searchingly, and then paced around the living room, past Sharon into the kitchen area, and back to his easy chair, babbling incoherently and slamming his hands into his pockets as if they were pesky appendages that had to be hidden.

And then there was Pip, the youngest and lowest functioning of the group, in her usual place, on the loveseat across the room from Sharon, head cocked to one side, left hand supporting her chin, in some ironic imitation of Rodin's *Thinker*. She resembled all of us and resembled us not at all: the same hazel-brown eyes as my father and me, but filmed and vacant, the thick brown hair of Luke and my mother, but twisted back into a tight French braid by Barbara or one of the other female aides so she couldn't suck on it. She was thirty now, less than two years younger than me, but her soft pink sweater and designer jeans seemed closer to teenager than adult.

As I drew near the love seat, Pip sprang up and headed past me toward the kitchen, walking sideways, shoulders sloped, left arm stiff and bent, hand hooked, the same way she'd walked since she was a kid. Really, she hadn't changed all that much, except for her face, which had lost all traces of baby fat and her slump, which had grown more pronounced.

A shiver went through me. It was worse than my initial dread. Not only were we both permanently damaged; we were also deteriorating.

I glanced at my watch, trying to manufacture some excuse to leave. Where could I say I had to go? Nowhere. *Fifteen minutes*, I said to myself. *I'm out of here.*

"Debbie," Barbara said, raising her head from the coupon section of the *New Haven Register*. She was stationed on a bar stool at the island that separated the kitchen from the living room. "Debster, Lisa's here. Why don't you have a nice visit with your sister?"

Pip shambled back to her loveseat with a fistful of potato chips and lowered herself, crossing her slender legs. As if trained at a finishing school, she refrained from eating until she was seated, and munched, slowly, meditatively, a connoisseur of junk food.

Was that what dissipated my urge to escape, that had me settling beside her? Her unwitting poise? Her innocent charm? Or was it the beguiling possibility that I, because of our common affliction, would be the one finally to break through the impenetrable to the person inside? Even if I did nothing else in whatever time was left to me, there would be that.

"Hey, Pips," I said, draping my arm around her rounded shoulders as I took her bonelessly indifferent hand. "It's Lisa." I looked straight into her blank eyes. "Your big sister Lisa."

She turned her head away and folded her hand under her crumb-speckled cheek.

"Oh," I said. "I get it. We're being coy today. Alright, Miss Coy. Then we'll just visit and catch up on everything."

For an hour or so, the two of us sat in the muted light of the living room, sunk into the pillows of her loveseat, its springs long ago collapsed from her bouncing up and down in response to some unknowable impulse. At first I talked to her just for the sound, inquiring about the ice cream social that Barbara told me she would attend that weekend. "What are you gonna wear to this social, Pip?" I asked, my words ricocheting off her face. "Hey, Pip," I continued, rubbing her plump, soft fingers, "I saw the nicest leaves on my walk here, all sorts of colors, scarlet and gold and orange and—"

At which she erupted into a snorting, seemingly joyful laugh only to withdraw into herself just as suddenly, the *tunk-tunk-tunk* of James's chair and Sharon's mumblings and the prattle from the television filling the silence.

"In a way, you and me, we're in the same boat, little sister," I said in a low voice while Barbara prepared lunch, appreciating, in a way I had never before, that I could talk to Pip as one might a gravestone or a pet, as a way to sound out thoughts that I wouldn't reveal to anyone else. How freeing it was, not to worry whether she had a clue what I was saying or that she'd broadcast it to anyone else. How odd, that it had escaped me until then. "Except, maybe, just maybe, I have a chance," I heard myself saying, patting her leg.

A smile lighted her face.

"Maybe. We'll just have to wait until the second of December."

Pip rolfed a laugh and looked away.

I can't say whether it was coincidence that a day after my visit with Pip, following another trip to the blood lab, someone from the oncology department called to schedule my third round of chemotherapy. Nor for that matter can I attribute with certainty the rise in my blood counts to any of the various measures I had taken to augment their numbers.

What I know for sure is that during the time I spent with my younger sister, I did something I had been unable to do for over a week: relax. Perhaps Dr. Chang—and Luke—had it right after all.

III

I turned around; no one. Not a sound, except the dock creaking, the water lapping onto the marsh beyond the NO OUTLET sign. The air went out of me. Every part of my body ached. Every muscle was telling me no more. *Steady*, I breathed, imagining myself limping across the finish line at twilight. *You're okay. You're okay. You'll figure this out.*

I retraced my steps. But then I got confused. Every street looked familiar until it didn't. And still no one. Houses everywhere but eerily quiet and shuttered.

An elderly woman, her snow-white hair twisted into a chignon, was trimming rose bushes at the edge of the vast garden on the side of her property. A white scar with a purplish tint covered one side of her face. A burn?

Later the scar would come back to me. As would my great aunt Adele's words the night after my chemotherapy had been postponed. "Lisa," she said once I had finished grousing about Luke's maddening complacency. "I don't expect you to take this in right now. But I want you to remember it. It's a Yiddish saying. *Iz tsures unter alle decher.* There is an ache under every roof. You hear me? Everyone has their own troubles."

That my sister was also struggling I never considered. Through those five months, my only concern was myself. I didn't know for years what she wrote in her journal around the time of my diagnosis:

I need Lisa/need my close sister/friend/confidante... Who else could I share funny tidbits about Mom and

137

Dad with, or laugh about strange people from our past experiences, or call to come up with just the right word, or a book recommendation? This thing is indeed fucking UNFAIR!

Luke then. Beryl Barry in my final months at the firm enduring a bruising custody battle for her children. And in the years since, a friend whose mother was killed in a car crash. Another with a baby son suffering from a life-threatening heart disorder and a mother with early-onset dementia. Speedo guy with his flat tire. The old woman in her garden now. There are no points for higher degree of difficulty, no way to quantify human suffering. And Adele had it right. I could never have grasped it back then. I was too deep inside it.

A left; a right; a stop sign; a turn; then the main road, she told me, quizzically regarding the racing number pinned to my T-shirt. I took off at a sprint toward who knew where.

There's something exhilarating about being lost. But only in the memory of it. In knowing you eventually found your way.

And only if you didn't try to get lost. Only if you didn't not let yourself flit away to a place so far gone that no one can find you, least of all yourself. Unless, in other words, what you were really doing was preparing to disengage for good, following the ancient rituals of the aged who go off into forests or drift away on ice floes or retreat to mountaintops.

Or, as I did in the final weeks before the December 2 MRI, performing the modern equivalent, wandering into the flickering maw of the television.

There's nothing exhilarating about that, even in the memory. Nothing remotely pleasant in revisiting those drawn, darkened days.

Until, that is, the bright lolloping six-year-old voice of my half-sister Marjy comes back to me, stirring me from my torpor. She was calling about Thanksgiving dinner at the home of Joan and Gordon, longtime friends of my father and Christiane. The dinner was two nights away.

"Please, Leelee," she was saying. Maggie would be there. And we could play with her but only if we didn't get her too excited. Maggie, it turned out, was Joan's ancient sheep dog. "It's going to be so great, and you can come in the car with me and Daddy and Mommy." Marjy was oblivious of the coolness between Christiane and me. If it was still cool. I hadn't seen Christiane for months. "Say you'll come, Leelee."

"Wait a minute," I said, feeling around for the remote and muting *The Real World*. I pushed myself up on the couch. Three or four recent issues of *People* and *Entertainment Weekly* spilled off the rumpled blanket onto the floor.

I'd been there for a while that day, had been there for most of the last two weeks, ever since a few days after the much-delayed third round of chemo, when the *tk tk tk* of the porcelain clock above the piano sounded the countdown to the second of December, with nothing—no more appointments, no more treatments—between then and the MRI, with each *tk* closing the gap between then and it. "Are you sure you have the right number? Because there is no one named Leelee at this residence."

Marjy squealed. "Leelee, stop kidding. It's you, Leelee."

"Okay, I'm beginning to get this," I said. "So I'm Leelee and you want me, Leelee, to spend Thanksgiving with you, Marjy, and a hundred-year-old dog Maggie. This wouldn't be the same person who makes lovely cards?"

"Yes yes yes yes I made that card," said Marjy. "And yes there's also going to be lots of very very very nice people and really really good food."

"Give me one moment to think this over, my friend." On the screen, a group of telegenic twentysomethings, sprawled in various attitudes around a pimped-out living room, engaged in glazed-eye conversation. I identified with them; they validated my sloth.

Not that I felt any guilt over languishing in front of the television for hours. What was the alternative? Sit around and wait for ghastly images of my August MRI to rise and burst forth, of being trapped in a small, enclosed space, of the sound of my cries being drowned out by the monstrous swell of the machine? Or of the MRI scan showing the tumor doubled in size and mass, with blindness and insanity just around the bend? Sit around and wait for my fears to send shivers through my body, to quicken that insistent pressure on the right side of my head, to reduce me to a blubbering infant in need of comfort and assurance from whom—my mother? my father? Luke? No. I'd troubled them enough.

This was better for everyone, I told myself each day as I flicked on the television, earlier and earlier. Better for everyone if I toughed out these last days on my own. And so it went: docudramas, reality shows, football, music videos, scandals—it didn't matter, so long as it was there when rumblings of dread signaled me to seek cover.

"You have to come," Marjy was saying. "You have to."

I hit the OFF button. Before Marjy's call, I'd pretty much decided against accompanying my mother to the Stamford waterfront estate of Cary's aunt and uncle, along with a gaggle of their friends and relatives, including Helene, a tradition in recent years, given the easy trip from Grand Central.

Better to stay home with Moose, some shiitake-mushroom stuffing and a *Thelma and Louise* video, even if it meant missing Luke and Cary; they had to head back to Baltimore that night. Better than subjecting myself to a group of people who knew me only as the New York lawyer who was Cary's sister-in-law, one who inevitably would be asked to recount her latest litigation war story.

This year, though, I wouldn't have any stories. I wouldn't be breezing in straight from the office, brimming with energy. I would be driven by my mother from her house, with half an eyebrow and a hat covering the bald top of my head. Not to mention facing everyone else, all of whom no doubt had been apprised of my condition, enduring their quiet pity and the furtive glances measuring the change the disease had wrought on me. "Let's give Lisa the seat of honor," I imagined someone proclaiming, as if it were the next best thing to a free trip to Disney World. Or, "the most tender cuts of turkey—where's Lisa?"

I shuddered. Moose jumped from the couch, skidded onto one of the magazines on the floor, and disappeared out the door.

"And Joan said we could play with Maggie but we have to be careful because she has to go for some surgery or something because she's always—" Marjy tittered, her sharp breaths jutting into the sentence—"peeing all over the floor."

I didn't tell Marjy that I had never taken to elderly incontinent sheep dogs. Or that I had settled on spending Thanksgiving alone. I didn't want to disappoint her. The night before my surgery, Christiane had bent over my hospital bed and whispered something about Marjy. What I remembered was her perfume, not her words; it exuded affluence and power. I'd asked my sister about what Christiane said on our walk the last night of the August week she and Cary stayed with me. "She said how important you were in Marjy's life," Luke told me.

To be sure, the grim nature of my condition had likely forced that admission to the surface; I'd said as much to my sister that night. And yet, those words, heightened by the cool reserve my stepmother routinely practiced in my presence, had not left me. Was it a leap of logic to assume that, through my closeness to Marjy, I had become special to Christiane as well?

Marjy was talking to someone, no doubt my father, at the other end of the line. "No, she's thinking . . . I'm not . . ."

I fiddled with the remote, my mind still on Christiane.

At times I'd found myself wondering whether she had been cornered into going to my apartment that early August day—she was the only family member in New York, after all, and in light of our history, it was more likely that she was motivated out of wifely duty or love for my father than anything that involved me. And yet there could be no denying that she had shown bravery, not knowing what she might find.

"Okay, I'll be quiet, but it would just be so fun," Marjy was saying in a lower voice. "Leelee? Are you there?"

"I'm here." I had no idea how much Marjy knew about my condition. She must have sensed something was off: I hadn't been stopping by, as I used to after a trying day of work, to help her dress up Barbies or draw pictures or have running races up and down the hallway. Then I thought of the card. It was just as possible she did miss me coming around without knowing much more.

"Leelee?"

"Still here," I said. Being with Marjy revitalized me, made my cares seem as neurotic as they often were; that was why I used to visit her after work. If she had any inkling that something might be growing in my brain that could kill me, it wouldn't just terrify her. It would compromise our easy camaraderie, perhaps incurably so.

I stared at the blank screen, remembering the two of us walking back from a candy store that spring, picturing little Marjy biting her lip, her dark eyes grave, as she shrank back from a man with a scraggly beard ranting from a sidewalk grating on Lexington Avenue on our way back to the apartment. Was that what she'd do when she saw me? Would she retreat into my father's legs, just as she'd grabbed my hand back then, until he wheeled her around and guided her away?

"She's still thinking," I heard Marjy whispering.

Moose trotted back in and leapt onto the couch, curling up beside me. I rubbed her neck. Marjy sounded as high-spirited as ever—certainly not the tone one took with a sick person. Which suggested my father and Christiane hadn't told her much, if anything. If that were the case, it was a no-brainer. I needed to show Marjy I hadn't changed, even if it meant dislodging myself from the couch. It was the same act I had been performing for much of the last five months and had of late neglected: playing the part of a healthy person.

"Alright," I heard myself saying. "I'll go."

Marjy shrieked. "Oh Leelee, we're going to have so much fun. The most fun ever."

After we had said our good-byes, I leaned back on the couch and rested my eyes on the screen. All at once, it seemed unnatural, spending Thanksgiving by myself. Joan had been a colleague of my father's before taking a tenured position at a law school in New York. A Texan with a commodious personality to accommodate her zaftig shape, she would doubtless conduct the dinner with warmth and geniality. And Gordon, an investment banker in New York, was invariably affable. With a presumably large group of guests who knew nothing about me except I was a daughter of my father and happened to prefer wearing a hat, how could it be anything other than a welcome distraction?

"Mom," I called out from the study. "Going to Joan and Gordon's for Thanksgiving."

"What?" she called back from the kitchen. "Be there in a minute. Repotting a plant." She'd been understanding when I told her of my decision against going to Stamford with her, but then again I couldn't be sure of her reaction; I'd only seen her form in the doorway in the blue light from the television in the darkened room.

"Thanksgiving. Joan and Gordon's," I shouted back.

"Great. Need a ride?"

"No. Dad."

"Great."

"Yeah," I said, more to myself, envisioning myself in my lilac pants suit and the matching hat Luke recently sent up from Baltimore. I returned to *The Real World*.

The pants suit was a mistake. I had lost weight in the three weeks since I had worn it last. But I'd been unable to tear myself from a *Bonanza* rerun to get dressed; by the time I realized it needed to be taken in and was rushing around in futile search of a safety pin, a car horn was sounding from the driveway. And the hat wasn't much better: after hugging Marjy in the back seat and saying hello to Christiane and my father, I felt the prickle of wool on my scalp.

The four of us approached the stately Tudor in the brisk night, Christiane's heels echoing on the wide pavement beside my father, and Marjy jouncing ahead, the lights from the university winking in the distance. I trailed a few steps behind, furiously trying to contrive some way to fight the urge to scratch through the evening—a shower cap I could cadge from some upstairs bathroom? a handkerchief? Kleenex?—and to keep my pants up—a paper clip from Gordon's study? some twine from the garage?

When we stepped from the dark-wooded foyer into the sea of heads and thrum of voices in the brightly lit living room, I felt like a convict just released from solitary confinement, having lost all social bearings. I clasped Marjy's wrist and, holding up my pants with my free hand, fled the cluster of unfamiliar Brooks Brothers tweeds and Talbots pageboys, tramping through the numberless rooms in search of Maggie the sheepdog.

"I'm not sure this is such a good idea," I said to my youngest sister after we found the old dog sprawled under a work table in the corner of a tiny windowless room on the third floor. Marjy wanted to ride on her back like a horse. "You might just do her in."

I lowered myself into a rocker. The spindles of the chair dug into my spine. The room was dark and cold. A faint scent of urine commingled with the aroma of roasting turkey. I didn't want to move.

"C'mon, doggie, get up get up get up." Marjy crouched next to the dog and slapped her flanks ineffectually, her new black dress poofing out on the floor. Olive-skinned with round dark eyes and already long-legged and willowy, Marjy differed physically from her mother only in the length of her ink-black hair: Christiane's was short and styled around her face, Marjy's straight and now nearing the small of her back. From my father, she had inherited the ability to plead a case—she had staunchly refused to have her hair cut shorter for upwards of two years, despite Christiane's appeals—and the way her nostrils tented upward when she was exasperated or enthused. "Nice doggie, c'mon, get up, nice doggie."

Maggie blinked, glassy-eyed, and yawned widely, baring a crooked row of discolored teeth.

"Yuck." Marjy stood up and backed away, wrinkling her nose.

"I think that does it, my friend," I said, letting the rocker creak back and forth. "You gotta get that dog to stand up if there's any chance of galloping down the stairs with her." From below, there was an outburst of laughter, like the report of a gunshot. The hat was becoming unbearable.

"Oh well," she said, shrugging the puffed shoulders of her blouse. She fingered a coat of arms nailed through its center to the wall. "Let's go back downstairs. I want to find Mommy and Daddy."

"Go ahead," I said. "I'll be hanging out here with Maggie."

Marjy looked back at the dog. "Wait—is she dead?" She knelt down again and leaned over her, the floor slats squeaking under her knees. The soles of her patent-leather shoes were embossed with the words BALLY KID. "She's not dead," she said cheerfully. "At least not yet. Chest's moving." And she skittered out, the tinkling of ice in glasses and animated chatter drifting in through the open door.

I closed the door and repaired to the rocker, cursing the

145

wool in the hat as I peeled it off and ran my fingers gently over the soft skin on my head. I gazed past the mound of sleeping dog to the collection of fireplace stokers propped against the wall, and let out a long breath. Six days until the MRI and here I was, shivering in a dark room with an enuretic dog. I should have been at my mother's house, stretched out on the couch in the warm light of the study with my shiitake mushroom stuffing and green tea and the sprightly Moose, losing myself in the numbing rays of the tube—

"I'll be right back," a female voice sang out from the floor below. "I just want to see the new stenciling in the master bedroom. Bunny says it's fabulous."

A crescendo of voices rose from downstairs. Chairs squeaked. There was a stampede of footfalls. "I'm coming right down," the same voice said. "The smell is simply divine."

"She upstairs, sweetie?" My father.

"I'll get her," Marjy said.

"Leelee? Leelee?" Shoes clambered up the steps. "Leelee? Dinner."

"Coming." I put on my hat, balled my hand in one pocket to hold my pants up, and met her at the door.

"Everything okay, kid?" my father asked in an upbeat voice at the landing after Marjy had thrown her arms around him and dashed to the table. He was wearing a corduroy jacket and cashmere sweater and his graying hair was brushed back. He looked distinguished and happy.

"Fine," I said. "Just thinking some things through."

"I understand," my father said, patting my shoulder. His eyes went grave. He knew. We'd been talking every night and the most I'd say was I was fine, but he knew. Six days. The second of December.

Marjy was waving at me from one side of the long table, her face radiant under the glittering chandelier. She was pointing at the chair beside her.

"What an adorable child," said a gnomish woman on my other side as I sat down. She had a mole protruding from her cheek. A pocketbook with shiny snaps sat upright on her lap. "Just like a china doll. Is she your first?"

Marjy put her hand over her mouth and shook with giggles.

"A toast! A toast!" Large-hipped and avuncular in striped suspenders, Gordon clinked his spoon against his wine glass from the head of the table. "To my wonderful wife Joan," he said. "And to all of you. Thank you for being with us on this special occasion. And may it repeat itself for years—and years—to come."

"Hear, hear," everyone chorused.

I lifted my empty glass halfheartedly and fixed my eyes on the lavish flower arrangement in the center of the table. My father was in my line of vision and I couldn't bear to look at him with my glass raised, didn't want to see if he had raised his glass as well.

"You might want to clear next year with Joanie, Gordo," someone in a Yale-blue blazer called out. His face was florid and he was holding a glass with amber-colored liquid. "Or it might be more of a take-out situation."

Everyone roared.

I put down my glass. It felt as though something was creeping through my head—or was it the wool? Was the wool infested? Or was the infestation inside my head? I couldn't wait for the MRI; then at least I would know what I was facing, wouldn't have to obsess over every sensation. Then again, if it showed that the tumor had grown . . . I shut my eyes and blew some air through my lips.

"Shall we go around the table and say what we're thankful for?" Joan was asking, red-cheeked in an enormous flowered dress. "Let's do."

"Oh Joanie, too many people," droned a man with a gray buzz cut and calculated stubble. "Too many ever so slightly

147

tipsy people in need of sustenance. By the time everyone's done, half of us will be positively comatose."

Another burst of hilarity drowned out Joan's good-natured protests.

"I had intended to sell but everyone agrees the market's not tanking even with this impeachment mess so I'm going with my broker's advice to just hang in there," someone was saying in an undertone a few seats beyond Marjy. I concentrated on the gold and cobalt-blue bands encircling my dish. "Oh, but now look at that turkey. Joanie, you've outdone yourself yet again. Hear, hear."

"Well, I suppose it can wait until next year," Joan was saying to Gordon.

I caught my father's eye. He shook his head with a sly smile. No doubt he was the only person more relieved than I was. Christiane, beside him in a sleek gray suit, was looking at me. Or through me. I couldn't tell.

"You know what I've always wanted to do?" the gnomish woman said to no one in particular. She reached into her pocketbook, produced a compact mirror, and checked her lipstick. "Ice fishing," she said, her pocketbook shutting with a resounding snap.

"Lisa, white meat or dark meat?" Joan was asking, standing behind the massive roasted bird. Was she speaking to me strangely? Too loudly or too slowly? Like the doctor telling me I had a brain tumor back in August.

"White." My throat felt dry. The pressure in my head reasserted itself.

Marjy tugged on my sleeve. "Gravy, Leelee. Gravy."

"Here you go, dear," said the gnomish woman. She passed the gravy boat over me to Marjy. "What a nice girl you are."

"Right," Joan was saying. "That young woman, the one in the hat."

Someone placed before me a plate groaning with food.

"Gorge away," he said in a phlegmy voice.

"But Professor Reisman," a bearded man with rimless glasses was saying to my father across the table. Christiane was patting her mouth with a napkin. "The right to privacy?" His mouth was full. He swallowed. His mouth was still full. "Should it extend to public figures?"

I took a bite of butternut squash bubbling with brown sugar. It melted on my tongue, sweet, smooth, rich. I wanted more. Why not? It was Thanksgiving, after all. But tumors feasted on sugars, I recalled hearing. I put my fork down.

"Oh well, there goes my diet," I heard a woman saying. All I could see was the back of her coiffed bob. "But anyhow, that's exactly my point, why do Americans always think they should feel *guilty* about their *things?* I'm the first to say I love our things, but Charles has suddenly gone so *Gandhi* on me . . ."

Fifteen or twenty minutes of the same and I excused myself, making my way around the table, through the kitchen, and into the bathroom where I let my pants drop to my hips, tore off my hat, and plunked myself down on the toilet-seat cover. I leaned my elbows on my knees and let my eyes rest on an adobe-colored tile, still tasting the butternut squash, my hands pressed to my pounding head.

This couldn't be good, my rising sense of discomfort, my revulsion at the rank superficiality around me. But were they all so superficial? As shallow as the guests seemed, could it be that I envied them, envied their inane concerns, their unapologetic materialism? Who wanted to be one of those people who finally appreciated all that was simple and unvarnished in life while staring mortality full in the face? No longer I; no way. I wanted to try ice fishing. I wanted to worry about the stock market. I wanted to wonder whether I should feel guilty about the things I had. I wanted the time to do all that. I wanted more time.

"Joan, the pine nuts in the stuffing—wonderful touch." Christiane's velvety accent amid the clatter of dishes. The two of us hadn't spoken or for that matter acknowledged each other throughout the evening. But there was something in the way she regarded me while we were at the table that signaled any further discussion of that Monday in August was taboo.

And it wasn't only Christiane who wanted the matter closed. I was avoiding eye contact too, and for a simple reason: I was ashamed. My stepmother had seen me not only unconscious but in soiled sheets drenched in urine.

In a perverse way, I had finally found my revenge—I had forced the woman I blamed for breaking up our family through the ordeal of finding me, of enduring the possibility that I might die on her watch, first in the ambulance, then as I hovered between life and death in the emergency room; forced her to suffer a trauma that haunted her for I didn't know how long—not deliberately, of course, but still I was the one.

"Cognac in the living room," Joan sang out.

I stood in front of the gilded bathroom mirror and studied the grayish cast to my skin, my haggard features. Yes, she had saved my life but that would be as far as it went. We were on opposite sides, Christiane and I. Christiane viewed my mother as my father did, as one to be scorned. The divide between him and my mother—and, given the allegiance I felt to my mother, between Christiane and me—had grown too wide, its elements too toxic, for even an act of such magnitude to bridge it.

"Oh, alright, and cigars for the boys . . ."

"Hear, hear," someone shouted above the din.

Cigars. Cognac. It was winding down. I pulled my hat tightly over my head and checked the pencil on my right eyebrow, which hadn't shrunk for a while, and then, as I had learned in yoga class, opened my mouth wide, sticking out my tongue as far as it would go, and gutturaled a quiet but forceful "aghhhhhhh." *Final stretch,* I said to myself as I crossed back through the kitchen and into the living room, hand in pocket to hold my pants up, sliding a leather-bound book from a shelf on my way to a chaise longue in the back corner.

"Hello there," said a voice laced with William-Buckley languor over my shoulder as I was passing the fireplace.

I halted and turned around. A silver-haired man, tall and lean in a smoking jacket, stood before me, listing slightly. He was holding a stoker. "Hays Johnstone," he said boozily. "Old friend of Joanie and Gordo's. From Greenwich." He shoved a few ashes toward the fire before returning the stoker to the brass stand and joining me against the mantelpiece. "My wife Bitsy," he said with dreary indifference, jutting his chin in the direction of a size-two blonde in a tailored black pants suit gesticulating to another size-two blonde in a tailored black pants suit.

"Sumptuous dinner, wasn't it," he continued. It wasn't a question.

I nodded yes. The sweet aroma of cigar smoke wafted toward me.

Maggie straggled in and sank down by the fire. Where was Marjy?

"You a student of Joanie's?" he asked. Something about the aggressive nature of his interest put me on guard.

A log collapsed in the fireplace.

"Actually I'm already a lawyer," I said, instantly regretting my words. I looked at my watch. "But, actually, if you'd you excuse me—"

"You're in the city?"

"No," I said, scanning the room again for Marjy or my father or even Christiane. "I was. But if you'd excuse me, I really—" I set the book on the mantelpiece.

"Aha," he breathed. He gaped at my hatted head over the half-glasses that rested atop the scrimshaw of blood vessels on the tip of his nose. "You're the one with the brain tumor— Joanie told us about you." His words seemed to carry as if the room had the acoustics of Carnegie Hall. "Hm," he continued, shaking his head. "Bad break." He cut his bloodshot eyes from

151

the party to mine. "Y'know, my sister died of a brain tumor. Happened real quick. Nothing they could do." He shook his head again. "How much time they givin' you?"

My cheeks went hot. "I don't—they haven't . . ." Nothing they could do. I felt a whoosh go through me, the floor giving way. I leaned against the mantel for support. The room seemed to swirl. "But they really don't . . . they don't know for—" I couldn't finish the sentence; how could I? How could I correct him when I didn't know?

"Lise!" I looked up. My father was in the entrance hall motioning to me and tapping his watch. "Excuse me," I choked, not looking back at Johnstone. I moved toward my father, limply, the waist of my pants dropped to my hips.

"Everything okay?" My father handed me my coat. "You look a bit pale."

"Fine." I was still reeling. "I don't know . . . " I tried to steady my voice. "I guess I'm a bit out of practice for social occasions."

We stepped into the crisp night air. The trees rustled softly. There was a faint smell of chimney smoke. Marjy was tripping ahead on the front path, holding Christiane's hand.

I pulled my jacket more tightly around myself. "It's just—you didn't mention to Joan—"

"What?"

"Nothing." There was no point in upsetting my father, or, more likely, incensing him, not yet, not when no one knew what would happen, when anything suggested could ring like the truth, not when I felt so fragile, when it was easier not to speak or think or feel . . .

Marjy darted back. She was wearing a camel hair coat, a smaller version of Christiane's. "Leelee," she said, nostrils flaring. "Let's skip all the way to the car." She had just learned how to skip. Christiane's Mercedes sedan was parked about fifty yards down the wooded street.

"Wasn't that fun, Leelee?" she said, taking my hand. From a distance, a dog barked, a clear sharp bark, cutting into the hush of darkness. "Didn't I tell you?"

"Yep," I said. "Fun." I suddenly needed to run. "Let's not skip," I said. "Let's run. Let's have a race. To the car." And before she could say anything, I let go of her hand and took off, my arms pumping, legs lengthening with every stride, my breaths coming jaggedly in sobs, running, running, running into the cold black night.

IV

Pain knifed through my side. I was sucking air, shuffling. But I was back on course.

I had followed what I took for a shout in the distance. Another stretch of seemingly endless road; no one. I kept going. Then, a clap, a voice, the scent of saline in the air, the majestic echo of the sea. I let out a cry of exultation. I was nearing water. The Sound. The Sound ran alongside the main road. The road to the finish line. One-and-a-half miles. I had lost seven or eight minutes, I figured out later.

Once on the main road, I was spent. Moments like that, moments when I had nothing left, I reverted to old tricks. This one: concentrate on the next telephone pole. Get there and I'd be that much closer. And because I was that much closer, there was that much more reason to reach the one after that.

Telephone pole by telephone pole. Break it down into manageable distances, my cross-country coach would say. *Point by point*: the slip of paper taped to the top of my law firm computer that I stared at in the early-morning hours to get to the end of a brief. Walk to jog to run. Andante to allegro. And lately—in the midst of my triathlon training, in fact—*graf by graf* to finish a rough draft of an article. *Get to the first buoy.* What, until my work as a reporter, had been missing since the end of my treatments. What would be my mantra, whatever life threw at me.

Just get to the next telephone pole, I told myself. *Just keep going.*

"Lisa! Lisa!" High-pitched children's voices. In the distance, the tiny figures of my niece and nephew on the side of the road were jumping up and down. Luke was behind them, her back turned to me, talking to someone.

Just as she was wheeling around, I picked up the pace. I was grinning like an idiot. Grinning through the pain. Better to smile than grimace when you're hurting, my cross-country coach would tell us. Smiling is a natural pain-killer, he claimed. Releases endorphins. Just don't abuse it. Just say no, if you know what I mean, he said, a twinkle in his eye; this was during the Reagan administration. Only force a smile when *in extremis.*

Except I wasn't forcing anything. I was smiling because I was thrilling to the sight of the three of them being there, seeing me, seeing what I was about to do.

I went past another telephone pole, past a waddling middle-aged guy, heaving, as if he might keel over. He wasn't giving up, though. Anyone could tell that.

Because it's not so easy to give up. Not in anything that matters. Especially beyond a certain point. Especially when your journey is freighted with the expectation of the people closest to you that you go on, no matter the struggle. Not so much from any strength or courage. Because it's the only option.

I didn't watch television on December 2, 1998, the day of the MRI, but traces of its cathode rays still must have been in my system, the way everything assumed a hazy glow, the light of a fading dream. Or maybe it was the Ativan, member of the Valium family, two milligrams of which I had already taken, the first when I got up that morning, the second on our drive to Yale-New Haven Hospital that afternoon, my father and I.

My father—he was the one I chose to accompany me. Not my parents together. There was no way. Sure, they'd put on a show of solidarity, try harder than ever before, but there was no way I could tolerate that oppressive tension just beneath their gritted-teeth cordiality. Not when what I needed was a sense of calm, the equanimity that comes with feeling secure and protected.

And that I could get from my father more than from my mother. My father, the essence of gravitas. My father, of the smooth, sure gait, the redoubtable bearing, the austere features. My father, with the gravelly voice that carried sway without having to be raised. *Let my daughter out of the machine*, he would say if I panicked again. That would do it. Yes, this was the time for my father's quiet powers of suasion, not my mother's sympathy and understanding, not for her being there no matter what. That would come, if necessary, later.

"I think I want Dad to go with me," I'd told my mother a few nights before. I had wandered into the kitchen during a commercial. "Is that okay?"

"That's fine," she said, almost before I had finished speaking, almost as if she already knew. "Do what you have to do," she said, her long face expressionless as she wiped her hands on a dishcloth.

I felt an ache behind my eyes when she said that, nothing like the heaviness on the right side of my head that had been coming and going that week, an ache of guilt, of the certain knowledge that I had hurt her but there was no other way.

I went back to the study and the couch. *NYPD Blue* was over. The soulful eyes of Joan Baez gazed up at me from the CD cover on the coffee table. *Joan Baez Greatest Hits*—I'd slid it from the shelf once I learned from Luke that the MRI lab at Yale-New Haven could pipe music from the control room to earphones in the scanner. To muffle the noises, she said.

My mother used to listen to Joan Baez when I was a kid. She'd taken me to a concert, my first concert—I must have been in the fourth or fifth grade—and I was sure that Joan Baez had been directing her songs to us, my mother and me, and some lady approaching my mother after the concert and asking if she wasn't Joan Baez's sister. She wasn't far off, actually: same eyes, same spacious forehead, same pronounced cheekbones.

Hey Mom, I could have called out. *I'm going with Dad, but I'm bringing Joan Baez. I'm bringing part of you, part of us.* I didn't. It had been enough to tell her I had chosen him. Besides, I was too strung out from all the television, my mind too numbed.

It was easier that way, easier not to consider what she must have been enduring—she must have known what I had refused to hear, the fifty percent odds that I wouldn't make it past a year, the ninety percent that I wouldn't survive beyond two, must have known that the upcoming December MRI could signal the beginning of the end.

It was easier that way, easier to blank out the underlined words on the well-worn scrap of envelope I had spotted on her bed table earlier that week—Dr. Quigley's September admonition that DIAGNOSIS DOES NOT SIGNIFY PROGNOSIS—to lose myself in the vicissitudes of the characters' lives on *Melrose Place* so as to stop myself from wondering how often she had read and reread those words over the past months; to dam the flood of guilt at the distress I had caused her.

It was better that way, better not to reflect on what she had turned off or kept clenched up inside her just to maintain a semblance of calm, just to ride the lurch and pitch of my moods, just to keep going.

Whether I was feeling anything on the ride to the hospital—a shooting pain, a dull throbbing, that heaviness on the right side of my head—I cannot say. Nor do I recall what my father and I talked about or the color of the winter sky or the density of the traffic on I-95 South or our walk from the outpatient parking lot to the hospital.

I do remember the underwater dimness of the endless corridor to the MRI Center and the sound of giddy laughter vibrating like a Jew's harp—it could only have been my own. My father was making some joke—*I could use an Ativan myself,* he might have said, a shudder fringing his words. I was weightless, coursing forward without effort, coursing forward along that endless corridor.

At some point we turned left. Short hall; swinging doors; stout woman like a humped stone behind the front desk. She looked up, a kind, worn face.

"Reisman," I heard myself saying. "MRI at 4:15."

"Reisman," she repeated, drawing her thick finger halfway down the schedule sheet, her voice slow and deep. She pointed to a perimeter of seats in the weak yellowish light. A fortyish woman with stringy blonde hair pulled back in a severe ponytail was dozing, her head slumped to one side, one leg encased in a white cast extended on the magazine table. "Someone'll be right out."

We hung up our coats and settled into our seats. My father clicked open each side of his oversized briefcase, pulled out a stack of papers from its middle section, slid a pen from the inside pocket of his jacket.

I set my leather bag on the floor, glanced at the months-old magazines spread out on the wide low-set table, a framed print of hot-air balloons on the wall. There was a low, monotonous rumble. I let my eyes close.

One way or another, I had trained for the forty-five minutes in the MRI machine since September. I had spent hours under the blanketed coffee table in the living room to accustom myself to dark, closed-in spaces. Late at night, in the wee hours of the morning, I had visualized the process: removing my boots, lying on the pallet, clearing my mind as the machine entombed me.

I had a pair of American Airlines eyeshields express-mailed by Cary the morning before. I had the *Joan Baez Greatest Hits* CD. I had an extra Ativan in the pocket of my jeans. I had Dr. Quigley who had agreed to be available for an immediate reading of the scan. I had my father; Luke had instructed him to rub my feet as a way of reminding me, in the dark reaches of the machine, that I wasn't alone, particularly at the beginning and at the end, just before they injected the contrast that would enhance any areas of abnormality on the scan.

I was ready.

Strangely I felt flooded with something like rapture. In a matter of minutes, I would finally leave behind the months blundering through the shadows. Whatever awaited, I would come into a brightness, one either cruel or soft. Whichever it was, I would at last meet what I was fighting, adjust, and press on.

I was staring at the masthead of *Town & Country* magazine, letting strange names drift before my eyes, as if I were watching the closing credits of a movie on television.

The rumbling abruptly shut off. The tick of the clock cut into the silence. Ten minutes after five. Fifty-five minutes late. I wanted to smash the clock.

My hand mechanically reached for my bag. I fished around for my mother's cell phone; she was staying at her school in New Haven in the event she had to get to the hospital quickly. I felt its weight, let it drop.

None of this was part of the plan. Not the wait. Not my rising impulse to gather the magazines from the table into a pile and drop them on the floor to stop the woman with the broken leg from alternately snoring and smacking together her thin bloodless lips.

Nor my father raising his head from his work and asking, every five minutes or so, "You okay, kiddo?"

"Fine," I said the first few times, jaw tight, throat constricted, voice a raw whisper. And then about fifteen minutes later, gazing blankly ahead, "I'm dealing." And then a few minutes before, having just dry-swallowed my third and last milligram of Ativan, a small grunt.

I looked at my hands. My fingers were trembling. The sedative was having no effect. I felt sick with rage at my father's utter absorption in his work, his tranquil oblivion. What was the point of his coming? To edit that article?

The same as ever. My father, elusive, detached, so that much more coveted. My father, who had never offered to take me in, not even for a weekend, who showed up for appointments and treatments when he could.

Of course I would have asked him to come with me, and not just for the authority he commanded. It forced him into the crucible. It fed my hope that going through this trial together with him might make us closer in a way we hadn't since I was a kid.

A short woman in drab green scrubs pushed past the doors and through the waiting area, nodding at the receptionist as she hurried past. My father did not look up.

I gritted my teeth, fixed my eyes on the balloon in the print on the wall and tried to reason with myself. Was I asking too much for him to set aside his work, this once? I didn't expect him to put his arm around me. That wasn't his style. I just wanted him to do something to convey that this wasn't some quiet space that might as well have been a library. Sure, an hour late wasn't so egregious—maybe it was the standard wait for an MRI—but I still wanted him to be as exasperated as I was and to act on it.

"Dad," I heard myself saying, the sound of my voice coming as if from afar. "Dad," I said again through my teeth. "Can you ask what's taking so goddamn long? And while you're at it, if there's any way I could get another Ativan? A milligram? Ask for a milligram of Ativan."

He must have checked his watch because I heard him

muttering some expletive, *fuck* or *shit* or *assholes*; I can't say which, but I do remember a faint sense of satisfaction at the venom in his tone, the assurance that a pill was within reach.

He was gathering his papers, arranging them into a neat pile on the magazine table, setting the stack on top of his brief-case. I let out a slow breath.

"Excuse me," he was saying to the receptionist, rubbing his ear. His pants appeared baggy in the back, his tweed jacket buckled between his shoulders; was he thinner?—my mind went back to his worn look in Dr. Quigley's office months before—"my daughter . . . almost an hour . . ."

As if on cue, a bearded, shaggy-haired guy in green scrubs sauntered into the waiting area a moment later, flipping a clipboard around his index finger like a Frisbee. The MRI technologist.

I cringed. This couldn't be right. He should be but-toned-down, serious, professional. This was too important for anything else. "Rize-man," he said, casually mispronouncing our name. "Come with me."

We followed him to a wall of lockers by the receptionist.

"Metal," he said, his voice toneless, slack.

I unclasped my watch, slid off my ring, passed them to him.

"Earrings," he said. "Unless you want your earlobes torn off." He grinned. I didn't. My father said nothing. The guy stopped grinning.

I took off my earrings. My father gave him his watch. The guy dropped everything into a small container. I fumbled in my leather bag for my mother's cell phone, the edge of the CD cover. I handed over the cell phone.

He deposited the container in a locker.

I held out the CD. "It's crucial that this be played," I said, looking hard into his sleepy blue eyes—was he stoned?— my father's square-shouldered six-foot-one frame beside me.

"Crucial."

He nodded, adjusting his grip on the cover as if about to practice a forehand toss, then, appearing to think better of it, stopped midway, and pointed us, about twenty feet beyond the waiting area, to a wooden chair with a built-in desk. He handed me the clipboard and shuffled off.

METAL DEVICES IMPLANTED IN BODY?	YES	NO √
HEART MONITOR?	YES	NO √
PORTAL CATHETER?	YES	NO √
HEART ATTACK(S)?	YES	NO √
CLAUSTROPHOBIC?	YES√√√	NO
LAST MRI?	*August*___	98

I raised my head from the clipboard and studied the sign on a heavy steel door, as if it could tell me the date of my first MRI.

MRI LAB
WARNING: STRONG MAGNETIC FIELD
NO METAL BEYOND THIS POINT
SERIOUS INJURY MAY RESULT

The words didn't register.

I left the date blank and signed the form. My script was shaky. I closed my eyes. My lids quivered. My head pounded. My ankle knocked against the leg of the chair.

"Lise?" My father was holding out some dried apricots from a tired Ziploc bag. He leaned against a concrete wall, one square-toe Oxford anchored on his briefcase. His face looked sepulchral. His eyes were lined with red threads. They seemed to focus inward.

I shook my head. I wanted to retch.

I planted my elbows on the desk and cupped my hands around my head, rocking back and forth.

"You alright, kid?" my father asked, concern in his

voice. "You need some water?"

"No," I said without looking up. I was no longer angry with him. I was too fixated on the Ativan. I needed another before this went any further. "Dad," I began again, warbly. "Dad—actually—I'm freaking out. I think I'm going to need another Ativan. I think we need to leave. I—"

The MRI technologist reappeared. He took the clipboard. "Ready to go?" he asked, his dirty-blond head cocked to one side and a mellow smile on his face like Barney and the Dalai Lama all wrapped in one.

I hoisted myself from the chair with wobbly arms and followed the technologist into the MRI lab and down a long, dark hall. My father's footfalls echoed a few steps back.

The doors closed behind us with ironclad finality.

The rest I can only recall if I close my eyes and feel the elastic of the eyeshields tight around my head—could it distort the scan, I remember worrying as the padded table slid back into the tunnel; how could I have forgotten to ask? And then my legs jerking, my heart gonging in my ears and my breaths short, agitated. And someone's hand on my left sock, gently massaging, and my legs still twitching.

I braced my body and from some primitive place deep within came a plaintive call. I was calling out over the din, calling out for the music "please turn up the music I can't hear the music" and then I was floating on a placid lake and the dulcet sounds of Joan Baez were flowing through the darkness . . . *yesterday is dead and gone/And tomorrow's* . . . I took in her soothing tones, let them sluice through me, let them blend into the whir.

"THIS ONE'S FIVE MINUTES, LISA..."

Liquid soprano rising above the thrum. *Speaking words of wisdom, let it be* . . . I am eight or nine and looking over at my mother seated next to me in the outdoor theater and there is a look of peace in her face . . . *there will be answer, let it be* . . .

"TWO MINUTES" . . . *shine on 'til tomorrow, let it be . . .*
"YOU OKAY, LISA?

I'm okay, I said without speaking.

"Lise?" My father. Hands on my feet, lightly tugging on one ankle. I am skipping over the cracks in the sidewalk, past the green lawns and the stately houses, and my father and I are chanting Mary McCool. "Lise?"

"I'm okay," I cried out into the void. "I'm okay."

"TWO MORE, LISA...ONE MORE."

Someone took my wrist. Latex. Frisbee guy? "This is the contrast, Lisa." A steely odor. A sting on the back of my hand. A coolness traveling up my arm.

The whirring intensified. I felt a current sweeping me forward. And then there was silence.

We were back in the waiting area. I replaced my watch; the metal felt cool on my wrist. My eyes winked and squinted in the light. It was a few minutes after seven. I slid my ring back onto my finger and reattached my earrings.

The mop-haired technologist was handing my father our coats. The two were shaking hands. My father gave me my CD, started toward the exit, held open the door for me.

I struggled to see through the thick mist, to remember where I was, why I was there, where we were going. Legs rubbery, clutching my leather bag, I followed him down the hall.

"Shall we take the stairs?" I heard my father asking.

"Sure," I said as pertly as I could, with no idea where the stairs would lead.

We tramped up three flights, our shoes scraping the steps. The exertion began to clear my head. "Well," I said, slightly winded. "I guess I made it." The words chafed my throat.

"You did," my father said, his voice oddly subdued.

Another door, another endless hall. The sharp smell of Clorox. An industrial mop bucket.

A woman was springing up from behind the front desk. "Hi, Lisa!" she said, her bright tone clashing with the puzzled look on her face. She was saying something to my father about car trouble, about waiting for her husband to get off work.

My father was waving his hand, cutting her off. "Where's Quigley?" he asked, throwing our coats on a wheelchair.

"No, Dad," I heard myself saying. "It's Dr. Quigley." That was when it hit me with a jolt. This was Misty. She worked for Dr. Quigley. We were in the radiation oncology clinic. We were looking for Dr. Quigley. We still didn't know anything. We didn't know if the cancer had recurred, if I was about to be given my death sentence. I felt the blood washing from my face, a sudden cold draft rising from my chest, taking my breath away.

Misty was saying she hadn't seen him for a while, that he must have left for the night, when there was a bang at the far end of the corridor. Someone was tearing toward us, the door slamming back, his stethoscope flying up and down, his baritone voice reverberating all the way down the hall.

"Wait!" the voice cried out.

Dad? No sound issued. I looked behind me. The corridor was empty. There was no one behind the front desk. Where was my father? I retreated a few feet, a few more, my boots squeaking on the linoleum. "Dad?"

"LISA! WAIT!"

I stopped dead in my tracks. I stood there in the middle of the hall and all I could hear was my heart hammering against my chest and the sound of my own thoughts. This couldn't be good, his furious haste. The tumor must have grown to a point where I could keel over at any moment. He must want to get me into that wheelchair before I took another step. How large could it have grown in—what was it?—five months? That must have been the heaviness in my head that I'd been feeling all along, the tumor pressing against my skull.

And now his sea-green eyes, dead serious, coming into

view, one hand pushing away his hair . . . I wanted to leave. I couldn't move.

I tried to steady myself, tense my body for the blow. Luke, my mother, waiting by the phone, not knowing—it wasn't fair for them, especially my mother, who'd been through all of it with me, who'd been there all along. I pictured her pacing around her office in the empty school, clutching that scrap of envelope as she stared at the phone, and choked back a sob. What would I tell her? *It's not good*, I'd say, voice unwavering. *But don't worry, I won't stop fighting. You know me. I won't stop fighting.* That was what I'd say, even if it didn't matter, even if there was nothing anyone could do. And Luke? *Oh well*, I'd say, forcing a laugh. *You can't say I didn't try. You can't say I didn't give it everything—*

"Did you hear me, Lisa? You're okay. No new growth. You're okay."

I blinked. "What?"

"No regrowth, Lisa! You're okay." All sea-green now, right in my face.

And then I was calling out for my father, tears streaming down my cheeks. I didn't want to break down, wanted to keep my cool, take it in my stride. But I couldn't. This was my life. I was okay.

I found him halfway down a side hall near the end of the corridor where we had entered, knocking emphatically on Dr. Quigley's office door. I was crying, but I was laughing too, so my father knew. And this man who, for as long as I could remember, had expressed affection for me the same way, by pecking the very top of my forehead or patting my shoulder, opened up his tweed arms and wrapped me in a giant bear hug.

"Mom? It's alright. I'm okay . . . Mom? Are you there?"

I sat on a bench outside the hospital, my legs stretched out on the moonlit ground, my mother's cell phone cupped to my ear. My father had gone to get his car. The chill in the air felt good on my face.

Sharp intake of breath. Then a queer, barbed laugh. "The exact words. Tell me. It was Dr. Quigley, right? Tell me exactly what he said."

I couldn't remember the exact words. "It's clear, Mom," I said, shifting the phone to my other ear. "No regrowth. I'm okay. I'm going to call Luke now, alright? Then I'm coming home."

"Alright," she said in a near-whisper, her voice breaking. "Alright."

"All clear," I said to Luke when she picked up the phone. It felt strange to say it, as if I were trying on new words that didn't yet fit.

A siren sang out faintly in the distance.

"Yeah, baby!" Luke said. "I told you. I knew it." But then I heard something loosen in her breath.

Cary was whooping in the background.

"You're so full of it." I was starting to feel like myself again. "You're just trying to act like the know-it-all older sister."

The lights of my father's car beamed toward me from the end of the circular driveway. "Here comes Dad," I said. "You wanna talk to him?" I suddenly didn't feel like talking anymore. What else was there to say just then? The cancer hadn't spread, but that didn't mean I was cured. There were still no guarantees.

I got into the car and handed my father the cell phone. "Luke," I said.

"She did it," my father said in a hoarse voice, rubbing his eyes as he pulled away from the hospital. "We're okay."

FINISH LINE

I don't remember crossing the finish line. But in the final fifty yards, I do recall catching sight of my mother in the crowd. "This is for you, Mom," I cried out. "We're okay."

I'm not sure where that came from. Probably from some reservoir deep inside me that the force of sheer exhaustion released. She was the one who had taken me in, who sustained my strength, who cushioned the blows. She knew I'd be alright, she always maintained. She never let herself believe otherwise. And in the nine years since, pretty much the same. She knew I'd find whatever I was looking for. I just had to be patient.

She didn't hear me shouting to her at the finish line, she said later.

And just like that, it was over. Olivia, Luke's six-year-old, was hanging on me, putting my medal around her neck, skipping around. Luke was chatting with Myra.

Bespectacled Jacob, eight, rushed back, having studied the race results and calculated my individual splits. It wasn't that bad, he said solemnly. If I hadn't gotten lost, I'd have finished around 206 or 207.

"Thanks, Jakester," I said, but the numbers seemed irrelevant. It was just as Adele had it. Everyone has their own aches, their own struggles. Every one of the 300-odd competitors had to suffer. Everyone had to endure.

As I was crossing the lawn to retrieve my bike, an older man in a Panama hat, toting a portable folding chair, ambled by, the upward tilt of his head and stride reminiscent of my father's. I hadn't invited him and Christiane to the race. I'd wanted to. But I couldn't bear to face the disappointment if they declined, or if they did show up, the tension I'd feel among everyone at the finish line.

Really, my recovery hadn't changed much. There was still the same discomfort in the presence of my mother and father; the same chasm between Christiane and me; the same sporadic flares with Luke and my mother.

And the same need to leave a lasting impression, even it was only with a byline. No, I didn't wear a T-shirt that broadcast my survival but there was a story to be told—first, about the race; I'd see about writing it up in the paper that week. Then, perhaps, something longer.

I stood my bike upright, already feeling the gathering stiffness in my back. That would eventually fade, as would the terror of drowning during the swim, the dread of skidding on the road, as well as the frustration of getting lost and the panic of being lost. But I'd remember—how could I forget?—that I'd gotten through it.

It wasn't so different from those five months in 1998 when I didn't know if I would live or die. I had found a way through that too. Eventually, instead of running away from what had happened, I might draw strength from that. Maybe I already was. Maybe it was part of what had gotten me to the first buoy.

On our way to the parking lot, little Olivia handed me back my medal. It was plastic, with a glossy sheen.

I stood for a while, studying the medal, the symbol that I had the energy and focus to withstand the physical demands of a triathlon, that meant I'd accomplished what I had set out to do.

I wheeled my bike in the direction of my car, the faint sound of upbeat music urging the last runners in, contemplating what changes I'd make for next year's race, when it struck me: I couldn't celebrate each anniversary of my diagnosis competing in a triathlon that proved I was physically back. It wasn't enough that I had endured. That couldn't be an end in itself. My illness would always be a part of me. But it wasn't who I was.

"Catch you later," someone singsonged at the other end of the lawn as they were getting into their cars. It was a woman with a purple streak in her hair. The woman from the Cove Center.

And there it was, in vague outline, what I needed to do next, what I inadvertently had been preparing myself for, what had me already planning who I might interview in my write-up on the race.

I was physically better; now I needed to engage, to take risks, to turn the adversity I had faced outward. Now I could use the strength I had gained to make a difference, even if it was only in one tiny corner of the world. Maybe, unlike Prufrock, I would never see a moment of greatness, much less watch it flicker. But I could still feel the glow of enduring goodness.

Naturally, getting there would be messy and complicated, fraught with dead ends and false starts, same as before. And, yes, every day would be a struggle, not a manufactured one like the triathlon, but a struggle nonetheless. No doubt I would fall short, again and again.

But I could do it. "Hey Scoop," told me that. Like the race—like everything—I just had to keep at it.

I headed back toward the crowd.

Acknowledgments

Prodigious thanks to the singular Lis Harris, teacher, mentor, friend, for meeting me at the start and coming through, again and again, to the finish line and beyond.

I'm indebted to Georges Borchardt for taking a chance on my story, and to Outpost19's Jon Roemer for his keen intelligence, patient guidance, and meticulous attention to making it into a book.

Thanks also to my peers Shannon Barr, Mandy Rice, and Kamy Wicoff, for pushing me to pare it down; to Robin Lane Fox and Anne Greene, early champions, and Alice Quinn, unstinting advocate; to Martin Washburn for his ever bracing ideas; to Tara Geer, Pamela Kandzari Campbell, Marily Nixon, and Julie Cavanagh Homza, treasured friends all; and to the Cavanagh family.

And to Myra Shahan, Helene Gross, and Cina Santos for time and again answering the call; to Susan Braden of the light hand and lighter rein; and to Kathy Kessler, Don Rahl, Ricky Jordan, Patti Rahl, Bobby Torello, and Janice Ingarra for opening up the dance floor.

Deepest gratitude to my family—in particular, to my older sister and my mother for reading countless drafts; to my father for his abiding faith in this project; and, not least, to my little sister Pip who immeasurably enlarged my world without uttering a single word.

About the author

Lisa Reisman studied Ancient Greek and Latin at Haverford, Oxford and Yale, and law at the University of Virginia. She practiced law in New York for four years.

A Dean's Fellow at Columbia University's School of the Arts, she also has been supported by fellowships from the MacDowell Colony, the Ucross Foundation, and Wesleyan University, and a work study scholarship from the Bread Loaf Writers' Conference.

Currently she is a freelance reporter and manages a local band. This is her first book.

Lightning Source UK Ltd.
Milton Keynes UK
UKOW01f1147170816

280885UK00004B/51/P